Praise for **Water Bodies**

"A reminder of how personal bodies and remember them, *Water Bodies* is anthology focused on defining feature

T0266540

"This book packs a narrative, poetic wallop. Having such fine and powerful voices gathered around a single subject makes the rain want to come."

—CRAIG CHILDS, *Tracing Time*

"In this beautiful anthology, writers, artists, and poets capture the wonder and heartbreak of learning from water in a dry land."

—MICHELLE NIJHUIS, *Beloved Beasts*

"*Water Bodies* overflows with lovely poetry and prose that gives the reader a visceral sense of what water means in the arid West."

—JONATHAN P. THOMPSON, *Sagebrush Empire*

"These essays flow and rush and collect in pools of wisdom in a drying climate, reminding us that water is a blessing, and the wellspring of our soul."

—ELIZABETH HIGHTOWER ALLEN, *First & Wildest*

"*Water Bodies* is an urgent call to protect and love the lifeblood that pours across this continent."

—MARK SUNDEEN, *Delusions & Grandeur*

"*Water Bodies* offers deep insights into how water shapes our lives and nourishes our souls, as well as our bodies—through culture, need, ceremony, refreshment, and sustenance."

—NANCY GUINN, Bookworks owner

"Prepare for tears of sorrow and joy, for these captivating currents of poetry and prose will carry you to the essence of all there is. In this existential moment, Paskus's moving anthology calls us to embrace water in all its forms—and to savor, and save, all we can."

—SANDRA POSTEL, *Replenish*

"*Water Bodies* is an exaltation. Each essay implores the reader to recognize that the presence of natural water is as essential to the nurturing of the soul as it is to the physical wellness of living beings."

—MARA PANICH, *Fact & Fiction Books owner*

"These essays and poems ripple across legacies of the southwestern lands we have shared, for better and for worse, through memories of conflict and mismanagement, connection and protection. This clear-eyed celebration of our most vital life force reveals us to ourselves and embraces a new vision of belonging."

—RENATA GOLDEN, *Mountain Time*

Water Bodies

water bodies

Love Letters to the Most Abundant Substance on Earth

Edited by Laura Paskus

TORREY HOUSE PRESS

Salt Lake City • Torrey

First Torrey House Press Edition, October 2024

Published by Torrey House Press
Salt Lake City, Utah
www.torreyhouse.org

International Standard Book Number: 979-8-89092-007-2
E-book ISBN: 979-8-89092-008-9
Library of Congress Control Number: 2023952238

Cover art by Sarah Gilman
Cover design by Kathleen Metcalf
Interior design by Gray Buck-Cockayne
Distributed to the trade by Consortium Book Sales and Distribution

Torrey House Press offices in Salt Lake City sit on the homelands of Ute, Goshute, Shoshone, and Paiute nations. Offices in Torrey are on the homelands of Southern Paiute, Ute, and Navajo nations.

To a kiss in a river and all that came after

Table of Contents

1 — **Introduction**
Laura Paskus

5 — **The Current Dream of Rebellion**
Sarah Gilman

7 — **A Long View Over Albuquerque**
Maria Lane

17 — **The Water Carrier**
Regina Lopez-Whiteskunk

25 — **The Intentions of a Desert**
Santana Shorty

27 — **Black Rock Dam**
Desiree Loggins

35 — **What Emerges on the Other Side**
Chris La Tray

45 — **Lightweight**
Daniel Rothberg

53 — **Water Eats, Earth Drinks**
Sarah Gilman

57 — **The Undertow**
Laura Paskus

61 — **She Wants to Be a River**
Michelle Otero

65 — **A Letter from the Confluence of a Very Old River**
Aaron A. Abeyta

73 — **The Shape of Goodbye**
Christi Bode

79 — **River Song**
Santana Shorty

81 — **Letter Born of a Snowy Morning**
CMarie Fuhrman

89 — **Gallinas River Park: Rules and Regulations**
Leeanna Torres

97 — **Sade in the Pandemic**
Fatima van Hattum

99 — **Rillito**
Ruxandra Guidi

105 — **Ocean Cactus**
Santana Shorty

107 — **What We Talk About When We Talk About Waters**
Kate Schimel

113 — **Skinny-Dipping**
Luke Runyon

119 — **Contributors**

Introduction

by
Laura Paskus

*A*cross every divot and rise of the planet, we are witnessing what happens when fossil fuel extraction runs rampant, without pause or recourse, and when we accelerate development even as scientists warn it must cease. And everywhere we are witnessing how—despite our power and our hubris—water definitely shapes our ability to survive in the places that, over time, we have called home.

Where I live in the US Southwest, we have stretched even our largest and lushest rivers beyond their capacity to roar, or even slink and seep, across the landscapes they've licked and shaped for eons. We've torn river channels from their floodplains, and floodplains from their groundwaters. We've overpumped aquifers—waters that in some places took thousands of years to trickle and settle—then sprayed those fossil waters on forage for cattle or squeezed them into pipes for cities excavated into lands growing hotter and drier with every passing day. In other parts of the West—even those tucked into long-term drought patterns—atmospheric rivers and freak storms have reshaped watersheds and cleaved communities off from their pasts and futures.

There are important stories for elders, poets, artists, activists, journalists, and others to tell about all these events and their consequences. Each of us should understand our place within the larger watershed and world. But we don't actually live our lives at the scale of interstate river compacts, ancient aquifers, interbasin transfers, or thirty-year projections.

From my home, a mile from the Rio Grande in Albuquerque, I

1

sometimes drive to the closest edge of the Colorado Plateau, about an hour away. The landscape there smells of sandstone, piñon, and juniper. It's different from the cottonwood, Russian olive, and granite of home.

There's a small canyon—you won't even notice where it crosses downstream beneath the highway—that I've walked in every kind of weather, where I've watched waters slide from catchment to crevice, stone bowl to catchment, and finally soak into sand and migrate toward a tributary of the Jemez River and then, the Rio Grande. Even when the canyon is dry, waters are present in the chutes and ripples they wore in the eons long passed.

Looking down, I focused mostly on the tinajas and narrow sandstone pools, the largest of which has an ancient spiral etched into the rock above. For years, I knew when and where there might be tadpoles and the swimming snakes who ate them. I walked past generations of ravens born and fledged from a nest at a bend in the canyon. Lizards ran ahead of me, robins flitted from tree to tree, always watching.

Then, one day, I noticed distant ponderosa pines—single trees stretching from a west-facing outcrop of otherwise bare sandstone. Leaving the canyon and even the cattle trails, my boyfriend and I pilgrimaged to the ponderosas, to imagine what waters must have dwelled here when these trees were first born of seed centuries ago.

Here, water seeps from or is held in sandstone, and each spring or catchment nourishes one ponderosa pine. Each giant tree and its tiny pool contains a universe: As the roots of the ponderosas break stone into sand, they build soil for other plants to grip. There are buzzing insects, tarantulas, and wolf spiders. Out here, I've heard robins, mountain bluebirds, bushtits, ravens, and once, a mallard; sandy poolsides reveal the tracks of lizards, mice, snakes, and even mountain lions.

Each time I visit, I'm newly astonished. Seeing these trees that don't quite fit within today's landscape or climate, it's hard to understand how the system survives. But I know the waters have something to tell me about survival.

Likewise, beneath Abiquiu Lake, a reservoir in northern New Mexico, I've heard the Chama River murmur, recalling her past and preparing to reclaim her future. Whenever I dunk my head in the lake and hold my breath, I hear her waiting. Even when the Rio Grande near my home dries into heartbreaking stretches of sand and dead fish—when the river becomes a ghost—I listen for messages from below the sands.

Encountering each of these bodies, I believe that if I'm quiet and cautious and patient enough, I'll learn how to navigate a world in flux.

All these beings and bodies also remind me that waters aren't a "resource" to be allocated by negotiators and managed by engineers; they're certainly not commodities. Waters nourish living creatures, to be sure. But waters are creatures themselves—entities with desires, dreams, and stories.

In this climate-changed world, we live in an ever-tightening present. The past is not prologue and the future is uncertain. But if we listen to the waters, we'll find a way forward. And while we stare at the stars and dream of flying, it's in water's embrace that we float. In union with water, we cry, we are born, and we survive.

And that's why the poets and writers in this anthology share stories of places where we swim or pray, where we bathe or fish. The contributors whose words you're about to read are friends, colleagues, and people whose writing I've long admired. Working with each of them has been a privilege, holding them together in one place, a joy. As crucial as it is to cover how the changing climate is reworking entire river basins, oceans, and continents, the writers in this anthology remind us that the most important stories of water can be as small as water hissing on hot stones or drops falling from the sky. Most of all, we offer you these stories with the hope that you'll cherish your own, and that together, we'll all love the waters that sustain us, challenge us, teach us what it means to be present—and offer guidance for the future.

The Current Dream of Rebellion

by
Sarah Gilman

Do dammed rivers remember
the shape of their drowned islands?
the depth and braid of their buried channels?
Are they wishing,
under that slackwater,
to carve themselves anew?
Overtop these roads
strong-arm these houses
these gas stations
these endless and arbitrary fences
into the current
into the current dream of rebellion
and so wait patiently
for the hard rain
that always and someday
comes

A Long View Over Albuquerque

by
Maria Lane

I'm sitting on a cold rock outcrop, with a quilt of city lights twinkling between me and a black western horizon. Once a month, this is my favorite place to go before sunrise. I park at the dead end of a neighborhood road that peters out in the foothills of the Sandia Mountains. By the light of a luminous full moon, I make my way through granite boulders to a vantage overlooking the eastern seam of Albuquerque, New Mexico.

I don't know when (or why) it started, but watching the full moon set is a monthly ritual for me. For years, I have been coming to this exact spot to watch the silent moon swell and drop. I come sometimes with a friend or family member but usually alone. Some months, I venture to other places in the city. Often, I go out again in the evening to watch the moon rise just after sunset. But whatever the weather, I prefer this hill, these rocks, this perch. I know the moon can set without me, but I never miss it.

The trail to this outcrop is short but steep, and in just twenty minutes I'm several hundred feet above the trailhead. Below me, the city's edge runs ragged against the boundary of the Sandia Foothills Open Space, which merges upslope with the Cibola National Forest. These designations protect the Sandia Mountains' entire western face, the crest line, and much of the gentler eastern slope as well. Plants and animals ignore the boundary signs I passed on my way up the trail;

they have their own lines of division and territory. In the darkness, I hear scrub-jays, thrashers, and towhees launch a morning ruckus, inspiring occasional participation from backyard roosters. And as the first pale sunlight begins creeping into the sky, I pick out chamisa, cholla, and Apache plume on the slopes below me. On the way down, I will see rabbits, rock squirrels, and lizards. Maybe a coyote, if I'm lucky.

Raising my gaze, a sharp geometry of landscape control comes into focus. The chunky rectangles of Albuquerque's metropolitan jurisdiction burn brightly with streetlights and porchlights, security lamps and building signs, freeway exits and airport runway markers. The edges of the urban lightscape stand out against a surrounding, multi-jurisdictional darkness. Far fewer lights burn in Pueblo of Isleta to the south and Pueblo of Sandia to the north. I see no lights at all in Petroglyph National Monument on the west side of the city nor in the Foothills Open Space surrounding me in the east. My eyes also seek out those few dark patches within the city itself: parks, farm fields, open space preserves, low-density neighborhoods. The most remarkable darkness is a rippling route of black that cleaves Albuquerque's lights in two: a cottonwood forest runs north to south along the Rio Grande, pinned into place by a city encroaching from both sides.

As I watch the moon slice toward the purpling horizon, I sift through the echoes of a different solo pilgrimage from long ago. As a young teen growing up on Florida's southern Gulf coast, I went to the beach on many evenings to watch the sun set. It was a different century, a different celestial orb, a different horizon. But the quiet darkness provokes cartwheeling thoughts, in which morning and evening merge easily in my mind. High desert vegetation in the foothills runs like a ribbon of sand along the white foam edge of concrete-block backyard walls, and I see waves lapping against the edge of the open space. My high hill feels like a dune set back from the coastline, offering prime views of the changing horizon and the tumult of the city. The stillness of the distant Rio Grande forest among the lights reminds me of a winter sandbar, disrupting and dampening the steady waves of the Gulf.

My old sunset sojourn provided a regular exercise in independence and trust. My house wasn't very close to the beach, and my favorite sunset-watching spot was down south, out of view of the tall condos then starting to take over our coast. I parked my bike at the dead end of a quiet neighborhood street that butted up against sea oats and dunes. I walked up to find a soft seat facing west, where I could watch the sun on the waves and feel the ever-present wind. My parents knew I always stayed until last light had faded; they made sure I had a bike light to find my way home. Eventually, after I could drive, my brother and I bought a small sailboat that we trailered down to launch from that exact dune. Again and again, I immersed myself in those waves, that horizon, that sky. Lost in the western view, my thoughts often wandered to questions about where I would go next in life. Usually, I fantasized about sailing away for a life on the water. In my clearest premonition, I saw myself becoming an itinerant poet, visiting ports of call throughout Latin America and the Caribbean.

The hometown departure didn't go like I imagined, of course. After graduating from the squeaky bike to an unreliable car and then from high school, I made a five-year journey northward. I went to college, got married, and started my first full-time job, with no sailboat involved. Then my brother died unexpectedly a few days before his twentieth birthday, and I returned home in distress, making my way immediately back to the water. My husband and I bought a sailboat and decided to live aboard. We docked near the city marina, close to family and to new (land-based) jobs. Surging through life with the tides and winds, we started to heal, but we also knew the water wouldn't be our permanent home. Within two years, we sold the boat, said goodbye to my family again, and started a westward journey that passed through Texas and ended in New Mexico. I eventually made my peace with the idea of leaving the water behind.

• • •

But this morning I'm sitting again on a dune at the edge of everything, facing west and thinking about water. The moon slips out of sight quietly, like a partygoer who leaves without saying goodbye. I watch the space where it last glowed, a dark purple band shifting into rose pink.

In the distance, the sky's faint glow outlines the colossal hump of Mount Taylor (Tsoodził in Diné), a volcanic complex comprehensively gouged with uranium-vanadium mines and covered with a veneer of remediation projects that do little to quell residents' fears or desperation for clean water. To the southwest, the Magdalena Mountains block my view of the San Agustin plains, where a fifteen-year conflict is simmering over a proposal to mine aquifer water for speculative development. To the northwest, I spot the tip of Cabezon Peak, a rock formation that stands sentry for the "checkerboard" lands of the Navajo Nation, a quagmire of jurisdictional intersections that allow energy developers to exploit private lands and poison waters just beyond the reach of Navajo governance. To the north, mesas and buttes guard the flanks of the Jemez Mountains, where devastating forest fires have destabilized entire slopes and put centuries-old downslope villages and towns at grave risk for flooding and water quality degradation. I cannot see the reservoir known as Cochiti Lake, but I know its water is tested regularly for heavy metals, thanks to an upstream nuclear weapons lab that is ramping up for a major expansion in plutonium pit production. The water that runs past Los Alamos National Lab and then into Cochiti Lake eventually flows downstream to Albuquerque, and into the taps at my house.

Because I am a historical geographer, it's hard for me not to see this pre-dawn scene in a colonial light. To the north, south, east, and west, New Mexico's landscapes are shaped by a complex interplay between colonial settlers' impulse to dominate, generational residents' refusal to be displaced, and environmental conditions undergoing rapid change. Albuquerque is no exception. It was in the river valley just below me that Spanish explorer Francisco Vásquez de Coronado spent the winter of 1540-41 during a reconnaissance expedition. A nearby hill blocks my view of the national historic site memorializing his camp, from which Spanish troops attacked and burned Pueblo villages soon after raiding their grain stores during harsh weather conditions. Five decades later, the Spanish mounted a full-scale settlement invasion of northern New Mexico, only to make a desperate southward retreat in 1680 when coordinated Pueblo resistance drove them out. In the early eighteenth century, Spanish settlers returned to this valley, founding Albuquerque in 1706 between Sandia and Isleta Pueblos. Many more settlers followed, pursuing an uneasy coexistence with existing Indigenous peoples and with the changing river valley.

As lights turn off across modern Albuquerque, the road grid starts to buzz. Early risers make their way past squat cylindrical water tanks in the eastern heights, rushing downhill toward the outcrops of office buildings closer to the river. Earth-toned houses dot every available space in the city. To me, they look like coquinas and sand fleas on the beach, washing uphill in the waves before digging into sand at water's edge. A stringy seaweed of landscaping trees floats above almost every yard, providing stark contrast to the treeless scrublands outside the city boundary. On that distant sandbar of the Rio Grande, I can now see the color of the cottonwood bosque in pale light. It shifts like an ocean with the seasons, from light green in March to dark green by June, from golden yellow in October to coppery brown by November.

This river once ruled the valley. It flexed its muscles in spring, drunk on snowmelt gushing down slopes in Colorado's San Juan Mountains. It sped through the turns of northern canyons then widened and settled across this central valley, leaving silty gifts on its shores. But now, the river is more of an absence: of people, of seasons, of water. Watchful from my stony seat in the foothills, I cannot see the waters of the big river behind its green barrier, but I have my quiet-observation spots in the bosque, too. I know it is running higher this spring than last year, when its anemic pulse left the riverbed sitting dry in the Albuquerque reach for several days in July. I also know this year's raucous flows are an anomaly in our era of higher temperatures and shorter winters. During my lifetime, we will surely enter a dry-summer regime, where all water in the valley is shunted into irrigation conduits, and none is left for the great river itself. This is our colonial present.

In my classrooms at the University of New Mexico, I teach students to think about landscape histories, patterns, and relations. We talk a lot about colonial structures and their persistence in "scientific" approaches to natural resources. The modern practices of quantifying, abstracting, and dividing natural resources into consumption units—waters, forests, grasslands, minerals—emerged directly from colonial structures and policies. When American settlers arrived in New Mexico in the late nineteenth century, they quickly enacted the colonial impulse to control people and convert landscapes for settlement and profit. New technologies for water control enabled large-scale commercial development at the same time they supported rising US political dominance. But these benefits to the settler nation came at the price of massive environmental change and social disruption, both of which persist, in New Mexico and elsewhere.

In this century, the Rio Grande flows only when its infrastructure managers allow it. We have converted a living river into an engineering problem, a legal process, a paper entity, a number on a municipal water bill. Evidence of the conversion lies in the size of the city spread below my dangling feet and in the nonchalance of residents who daily ignore the river that supports their settlement. Every time we turn a landscape or a river into an abstraction, we make it harder to engage with it as a place where communities and relations can be founded or sustained. I argue that placelessness itself provides the mental cover and emotional distance to normalize colonial structures and inequalities. If a place has no inherent meaning, there's no moral reason not to remake it to suit our own comforts and desires, wasteful and destructive though they may be. I am saying "we" and "our" because I am a placeless settler, too.

• • •

The sky is lightening now, making its daily transformation to blue above Albuquerque's western mesa. Below me, I see a handful of tiny hikers, trail runners, and dog-walkers starting up from the trailhead at the dead-end street. I meet these people on the trails every month, and many of them look like me: white, middle-aged professionals. What are we all doing out here among the sage and sedge?

No, I never intended to move to the desert but, yes, I always intended to leave my hometown. In the white-immigrant settler tradition, each generation deepens its commitment to social and geographical mobility. My parents showed me by example how to live far from family, my schools prepared me to be successful anywhere, and my profession demands a willingness to move (which is ironic, since my academic discipline generates theory about place and belonging). But mobility always comes at a cost. By choosing to move for the best job or the amplest opportunity, settlers like me always end up in places where we don't belong. I myself long thought I belonged on that southern gulf coast and its waters, but I left freely and with focused intention. Twice. That is the essence of placelessness. You can always leave; no strings attached. Home is not necessarily the place you live, and home maybe doesn't even exist. No wonder settlers like to remake the landscape in every new location.

I never thought too deeply about my own placelessness and participation in settler colonialism until I began engaging with UNM students whose lives are anchored by ancestral and generational connections to New Mexico landscapes. I watched them wrestle with the excitement of learning new ways of thinking alongside the fear of leaving old ways and places behind. My own mother is an immigrant to this continent; you would think I might better understand the murky and painful transitions between generations and locations. But I never personally faced difficult choices between learning and place. Placelessness was just a fact of life for me, scary at first but easily swallowed when everyone around you is also moving mindlessly from one place to another.

• • •

The sun is high enough now that I can feel the first rays coming over the crest of the mountain. With the moon long gone, I hike down my hill and head home for breakfast. After work, I plan to walk on the riverside trail where I can watch the full moon rise from a vastly different vantage point.

As a scholar, I have long pondered the way settler governments and infrastructures change and control landscapes to suit the whims of people who won't ever see that place as home. All my pondering has left me with numerous unanswered questions. Is it possible to escape the settler condition? Can settlers ever remedy their complicity in the displacement of place-based societies and people? What would it mean to *generate* a sense of place and belonging, to acknowledge settler histories without re-enacting settler power?

I have started to turn the ship of my academic career toward disruptions that question settler science and challenge the ways it dominates academic institutions. My goal is not to destroy higher education, to which I have devoted my career and to which I will entrust my own children's future. But I insist we acknowledge that many institutions of "learning" impose narrow views of the world, especially when valorizing science. Through endless affirmation of STEM disciplines above other ways of knowing, we ensure that only a minimal number of graduates will be prepared to establish meaningful place-based lives and relations. We've instead encoded placelessness into knowledge, as if that's a solution to problems rather than a cause. Don't get me wrong—I don't want to eliminate science or engineering. But let's not forget that these things have histories, and they are not pretty. You can't look anywhere in beautiful New Mexico, even in the dark, without seeing them.

Next month when I make the trek again to watch the full moon set in bands of purple and pink over the sea of Albuquerque's predawn lights, I will reflect again on an infinite waterline in a different town, where other settlers have filled in the space I left so long ago. From the Gulf coast to the desert Southwest, and across North America, it is time for new modes of belonging that bind people to multiple places, knowledges, and social foundations. Like our dazzling lunar companion, let us embrace change in its many phases.

The Water Carrier

by
Regina Lopez-Whiteskunk

In Water
I am surrounded.
I am safe.
I am pure.
I am sacred.

*A*s I sit watching the beautiful blue shift to orange, and then yellow, I see a warrior take from his quiver a willow with an arrowhead and feathers attached. An arrow darts off to the cosmos. With the arrow goes my heart, and I recall a time of long conversations with my parents explaining to me what my responsibilities are to this world and family.

I came to understand water is life. Water is not to be wasted. We pray for it and with it. The process of gaining knowledge is the journey from a young girl into adulthood. Water comes from the earth in its blessed way, and we surround ourselves with ceremony to celebrate, embrace, and stand with gratitude for the water.

Before we enter this life, we are surrounded by the protection of water. Our mothers carry us for nine months nestled within a womb, our forming selves experiencing the songs of her voice, the drum vibrations of her heart. Just as our Mother Earth blesses our human existence with water, nurturing the land, becoming clouds to return water to her.

Water is life
We pray for water
We pray with water to bless our loved ones and all that is around us
Water provides for us
Water can take from us if we are careless.

I dreamed of a day to share my stories with my granddaughters. I was nine years old in third grade, falling off the monkey bars on the playground. I am now fifty-three years old and far from the elementary playground and the mean girls who never let me join their laughter. It was a Saturday morning when my mother called me into her bedroom, placed me on her bed and said weird things like, "You are becoming a young lady." She said that there are things we do because of the family we are. I was about to take my place. The preparation to become a keeper of knowledge and accountable for how water is used within our sacred ways and life as a Ute woman would begin.

My father was raised by his grandfather, our last medicine man for the Weenuche, Ute Mountain Ute, people. Serving others is a huge task. A healer lives a humble life spent serving, helping, and assisting others in their needs. What does that mean? One might think it is healthy and physically related, which is, in part, true. Spiritual and familial health are important aspects of the process of healing. As women, we assist in many aspects within that life of service, helping others and being good hosts. As a young lady, life was being exposed to me. I was gaining knowledge of my place and my honor to be Regina Lopez. The great-granddaughter of Walter Lopez, granddaughter of Jacob Lopez, daughter of Norman Lopez. And now I am a water carrier. I will see when I need to pray for, pray with, and serve others who need water in this life and after.

My mother was very calm and caring when she told me, "Your grandfather is going to be running a peyote meeting and wants you to carry water in the morning."

Oh! I will have to get up very early that morning. What will this all entail? What will I need to know? I was nervous. Will I be able to remember all that I need to do? I was under the guidance of an elder, who would instruct me for the morning. The circular motion, always turning to the right in a clockwise direction and keeping my mind and heart in a good place for the ceremony. Remaining mindful of every movement. I would be carrying a bucket of water when the morning star appeared and I would wait to be summoned by a whistle blown by the leader of the meeting, my grandfather. I would walk the bucket around the teepee, starting from the east, south, west, north, and back to the east near the door. This made me think about how sacred and special this moment would be. In life, we experience a world of firsts that our parents celebrate. First winter, smile, laugh, step. But when a sacred moment is experienced, that is our connection to the Creator. A sacred first is a commitment to serve when called upon. Becoming a water carrier for a ceremony was scary, but humbling. To know what I was to become that morning as I felt the brisk chill in the air filled me with honor. Water is an element that is necessary for life but is also used as a tool to protect and strengthen others. Other humans, animals, birds, insects, and all that is created by our Almighty. I was nine years old, and I felt like the center of the universe.

I am not an alternative.
My grandmother collected water
from nearby creeks to carry
back to our family. Was that an alternative
way to turn the faucet on in the kitchen?
When she collected wild onions,
was that an alternative
to going into the grocery store?
Harvesting the sage from the hillside
to soothe congestion was an alternative
to going to the pharmacy.
Was the love of the mountains, deserts, and valleys
a way of life or an alternative?

Overwhelmed with the excitement, I didn't need anyone to wake me.

I was lying in my bed when my mother came to my bedroom and announced my grandmother had arrived late last night to be with me. I heard a soft voice and then my name in our language, Mah mah tah pooch. Then her giggle when she pulled me into an extra-long loving hug. My mother and grandmother asked me if I was ready for this. Did I have a choice? In our culture and family, an honor like this is not a choice. I understood that from the first conversation with my mother on her bed. I was instructed to put on my floral printed dress with brilliant-colored ribbons. Moccasins fully adorned with a geometric design, and matching leggings that covered my calves. When my mother finished braiding my hair, I wrapped it with mink and placed my beaded hair ties on my braids. My grandmother placed a scarf over my shoulders. The final article was my belt that had a place for a small knife, awl, and pouch decorated with beads of the many colors that make up the sunset. I remember my father coming through the front door, looking for me, and saying, "Are you ready?" He took me to the ceremony location just below the mesa, where there was a house with a teepee set up for the ceremony. I lived close to the Ute Mountain, so it was a five-minute ride.

My father put a silver and turquoise bracelet on my right wrist. Then he shared with me a message from my grandfather: wear this with strength, and grace. My mother put a pair of silver earrings on me and wrapped me with a colorful Pendleton blanket with fringe. The Pendleton blanket was of wool with colors of yellow, orange, red, blue, and purple; it was an honor to have a blanket of this type. She instructed me to wear the blanket over my shoulders until I got ready to enter the teepee. Fold it and sit on it when I take my place in front of the door after I place the water bucket directly in front of me. My grandmother painted my face which made my cheeks feel the earth at sunrise: peach. She told me how the peach will protect, guide, and identify me when I am in sacred motion. With the gentlest touch, paint was placed at the corner of my eyes, on my heart, at the center top of my forehead, the middle of both palms, the back of my neck, and a dab on my tongue. She whispered in my ears, "You will do good!" They all showered me with hugs and smiles. In the dark early morning sky, I could see the sparkles in their eyes like stars leading the morning star onto the new day.

"Your walk is waiting, you need to go," said my mother. Grasping the bucket and embracing the gentle chill in the early morning, I took a deep breath. I was taking my position as a water guardian, voice, taking my position as a Ute woman in my family. Little did I know this would be the first of many lessons water would teach me. In prayer and sacred position, the water speaks. Water is all around us and falls to our Mother Earth in many different forms. Water flows through river beds and carves canyons of great depths. Passes through the land to vast oceans. Deep beneath our feet many rivers and aquifers provide support for life. Water tells us we do not need to see with our human eyes to know that life is all around us. The lesson of knowledge and relationship with water exceeds human awareness. As a young girl, my parents and grandparents brought me to the position to sit, listen, and learn from the element, open my heart and connection to take in the knowledge.

My grandfather, Jacob, lived in a small cabin with no indoor plumbing or electricity throughout my childhood. His life was spent moving with the seasons, moving his livestock to Ute Mountain during the warm seasons and off Ute Mountain during the colder months. Water to his life and animals depended on how the creeks and springs flowed. Grandpa Jacob, a gentle loving man who enjoyed his life with his animals and family. Slender and about five foot four inches tall, had the best laugh. A cup of coffee, cigarette, and gentle gaze told us we were safe in his presence. His role as a Sun Dance Chief was important to our people at the beginning of the summer moon. Three or four days would be spent in deep prayer, surrounded by song and dancers to the left and right of him: no food or water. Being the granddaughter of the Sun Dance Chief meant we cared for water mindfully. The men would pray for the people as their sacrifice. Their sacrifice was a fast which meant no food or water for the duration of the ceremony. Water again is the teacher, teaching one should be thankful for that next drink of water you are blessed with. In the chief's camp we need to keep all visitors, singers, and family members fed and offer water to drink. Fresh water is brought into the camp every morning; it's never wasted or dropped to our Mother Earth for the duration of the dance.

One afternoon my cousin and I sat in the lodge under the heat of the sun. Our cheeks were pink, and when grandpa called us to the center pole, he gently put his hand on our heads. He said in a low, loving voice, "Go back to the camp and cool off in the shade house. Drink some water for us all. Come back this evening." We walked back to our camp laughing. We assumed we had done something wrong, but it turned out he was proud of us for sitting the afternoon in the sacred lodge singing. In my grandfather's eyes, I understood we could do no wrong. Permission was granted to leave the sacred lodge to drink water for all the people.

Water
Element
Snow
Underground
Rain
Rivers
Lakes
Oceans

When the ceremony concluded, water was carried into the sacred lodge, and we sang the water song to announce to the world that this dance was completed. Our warriors have come through the three days without food or water. Watch them walk out the same way they walked in. Let this sacred journey be complete for the year. Water is placed next to the sacred center pole and first shared with the dancers, then the people. When we partake, we bless ourselves by placing water in our hands and putting the water on our heads and going down to our feet.

We then drink a sip or two showing gratitude to the warriors for their sacrifice and our Creator for water in our world. I listen to the prayers spoken, sung in songs, encoded in the dance rhythm, and in our movements each day of the ceremony. We are sharing gratitude for all that is shared with humans, animals, insects, and all that is around in our natural world. It amazed me how peaceful it was on the mountain in early summer when Sun Dance occurred. Living in southwest Colorado, we do not have a lot of water. We honor what we have.

Walking with Grandpa Jacob was always a big highlight but a more significant honor. As we got closer to our camp, our mothers, aunts, and other females rejoice with the lulus. Announcing to our relatives and all that is around, they are home! A little water was shared with Mother Earth. Off in the distance, I could see clouds gathering when grandpa said to my parents, "If you do not intend to sleep up here tonight, you might want to get off the mountain soon. It is going to rain." It was amazing it did not rain the whole time the ceremony happened. Later that evening, it rained just as he said it would. The celebration was enjoyed by all getting a drink of the precious blessed water.

Water is an element we pray for, pray with, and sacrifice for. Earth, water, wind, and fire are blessings. It is helpful to humans, serves our lives but also can be powerful enough to remind us when we are not upholding our responsibilities. The elements teach us every day in so many ways.

The Intentions of a Desert

by
Santana Shorty

Desert wants
We all know
What the desert wants:
Cholla yearn, prickly pear bliss, a cottonwood lullaby
The ponderosa pondering, the juniper daydream
Purple aster and cactus flower song.

Desert wants
An emblem of what if
What if I wasn't the desert?
What if the tundra ice didn't melt?
What if I was rainforest?
Was ocean floor?
Was an elixir paradise of fronds and moss and dew and forest floor
    and brash orchids and green spotted frogs?
Was seascape? The place of orca play and cephalopod meandering.

Desert wants
The sun, a little softer
The summer cloud, a little heavier
The winter snow, a little more often
Daddy to tilt his head to the sky, his thick hand shielding the worn
    light, and to say,
"There should be good runoff this year."

In our dreams, we see the skull cracked tooth in red earth and a
    chance to pick it up or walk away.

We see the petroglyph warning and we turn for home.

We see the tufted remains of a she-cow who fell into an arroyo crev-
    ice.

We see goat heads planted across the bottoms of our shoes and we
    are reminded of the stars.

We see the tumbleweed that should never have been here, piled
    against the barbed wire fence that should never have been here.

Desert wants, desert has, and desert will never be.

Desert wants

Juniper berry gin tumbler on the mesa cusp, on the rocks,

Delirium at seven thousand feet.

You are not drunk, you are just not used to this.

Not used to crying when you see a fiery pink cactus blossom set
    among the rattlesnake pit with tender raindrops clinging to its
    needles after a sneaky rain shower fell on only this four-foot
    perimeter where you stand,

Not used to calling fallen antlers among the pine needle turf, spikes
    pricking the sky, beautiful,

Not used to the feeling of freshly made mud between your toes and
    the wafting petrichor making you weep because your lips are
    cracked and your knees are ashy and you have never known the
    want of water until now.

Walk back to the acequia.

She will wash your feet and hand you a gourd.

You are welcome, now that you know our language of longing.

Black Rock Dam

by
Desiree Loggins

*N*early three years ago, my partner and I moved into the Pueblo of
Zuni's Blackrock subdivision, our home a stone's throw from
the Indian Health Service Hospital and several neighbors with homes
identical in layout and construction to ours. Blackrock, a place named
for basalt deposits left behind from historic volcanic activity, is small
and practical. There are several government buildings, a playground,
and short-term rental homes for tribal members and non-Zuni who
work in the community. The layout and construction of each house
and apartment is nearly identical, but each residence is set apart by its
view. By chance, you may see your neighbor's backyard, the highway,
or open sky and far-reaching mesas. By chance, our home happened to
abut the defunct Black Rock Dam and the trails that surround it.

The dam in all its overgrown glory, both constantly changing
and unchanging through the seasons, join my partner and I for dinner on our back patio and accompany me while I water the garden.
Having this unobstructed view from the intimacy of my home helped
the Black Rock Dam progress into a personal wonder of mine. After
I learned why it was there in the first place, I had endless questions
about what it meant for the dam to still stand in this community. And I
wanted to know what my lucky view could tell me about living with a
past that refuses to be forgotten.

A dozen or more tract homes sheltering IHS employees and Zuni
families line the dry dam impoundment on one side, while Highway
53 and a dense gallery of cottonwoods and aspens frames the other.

From my back window I can watch dusk cast a shadow over the dusty brown pit that at one point strained to hold the US government's paternalistic vision for Zuni's westernized agricultural future, a vision animated by the Reclamation Act of 1902.

The land rejected the dam only a few years after the "Indian Service" (now the Bureau of Indian Affairs) declared it complete in 1908. Inundated with heavy flooding, the concrete spillway splintered, and silt overload from the Zuni River prevented meaningful water storage. As designed, Black Rock Dam was incapable of holding enough water to irrigate crops. Meanwhile, its construction disrupted traditional agriculture, degraded acres of shrubland, and destroyed several sacred springs.

Now, the Tribe manages the care of this massive monument to Manifest Destiny, and today I walk its service roads in my sweatpants, collecting the sunflowers that sprout from its cracking foundation.

The first time I saw a herd of elk exit the tree line and stride toward the middle of where a massive lake should be, I pulled on a coat and ran to greet them, galloping across the spongy mat of bare soil and kochia skeletons. I felt lucky to witness my new neighbors.

From this wide-open vantage point, I could feel how the lakebed was vibrant with life and possibility, but also constrained under the weight of a massive colonial object. From here, I could see the dam's body, its towering gray walls and basalt-lined embankments, and beyond, glowing red mesas and silvery stands of coyote willow. A Zuni woman jogged by in the distance, wearing a flawless bouffant and waving on her way to a bridge that crosses the crest of the dam while a loyal pack of dogs followed in her path.

The Zuni people have persisted through two waves of settler colonial disruption of ther land. In the mid-1500s, the Spanish Crown's foot soldiers traveled from their settlements in the Rio Grande Valley to seek out gold and establish missions in remote Zuni villages. In rejection of Spanish intrusion, the tribe joined the 1680 Pueblo Revolt and successfully pushed their oppressors out of what is now New Mexico. After the Spanish returned to the area, the Zuni people consolidated from six ancestral villages into one at Halona:Idwan'a, about four miles from the mixed population suburbs of Blackrock.

Then, when New Mexico became a United States territory in 1848, a second wave of European colonialism swept through the Pueblo with even greater force and an intention to redesign traditional land-based lifeways to mirror its own idealized image. This meant coercively reorganizing Zuni's water future for the benefit of Anglo settlers and capitalist expansion.

My position as a guest living on Zuni land allows me to witness the Black Rock Dam with a curiosity and bewilderment removed from ancestral memory and loss. My fascination comes from its undeniable visibility and how it shouldn't only be looked at as a metaphor, but an active player in the community. Beyond history and function, the permanent concrete façade of the dam is also a skatepark for teenagers, a hiking trail, and a peak that coyotes gaze out from.

Daily, I walk the dam and observe its ecosystem as it changes with the seasons. I've become familiar with its textures and its regular visitors, human and non-human. My energetic dogs experience its inorganic infrastructure as a benign plaything.

Often, I struggle with how to think of the dam and what it has wrought—and I wrestle with the knowledge that I don't have to think about it, not in the ways my Zuni neighbors do.

I know what it is to live with the effects of colonial violence. It is in my blood, on my tongue, in the subtle features of my family's faces, and in how I feel when I am wandering on stolen land as a descendant of stolen people. Apart from the color of my skin, much of this can be obscured through purposeful forgetting, assimilation policies, and the overall success of Manifest Destiny ideologies. But the dam's physical form can't be obscured. The slow growing juniper won't cover it completely, and money and time have not been able to fix or reclaim this land for the Tribe's benefit. It stands before me, and I accept its constant influence on my movement and thoughts.

This is what preoccupied me about the Black Rock Dam. It is a large piece of failed settler infrastructure that continues to shape the landscape and experiences of people around it long into its afterlife. The Zuni people (A: Shiwi) and guests on A: Shiwi land shape the same landscape and experiences through their interactions with the dam, the surrounding environment, and with each other. The Black Rock dam is inextricably tied to its history and original construction, but the Pueblo is not a passive vessel receiving its intentions.

For most people of my generation on Zuni, the lakebed had always been dry. During summer monsoons, rainwater occasionally pooled at a low point near what seems to have been the intake tower of the dam. The water was always green and foamy and ultimately no more thrilling than a water-filled pothole.

New Mexico is in a perpetual state of drought and Zuni's own surface water flows have mostly dried thanks to upstream diversions on the Zuni River and climate-change-induced drying. Elders recall orchards and saturated earth, but the idea of abundant water remains somewhat abstract for young people and guests who are today pelted with dust storms and surrounded by dry arroyos.

According to the US Geological Survey, the reservoir had an original storage capacity of 15,000-acre feet in 1908, but by 1944, sedimentation had decreased the storage capacity to 2,600-acre feet. A Zuni community member eventually told me this had indeed been a lake in the 1980s, "Top Lake," a place where people would fish and take boats onto the water. Over time, the lake drained, then emptied entirely.

I grew up in California, but I have now lived in New Mexico long enough to know that each year, the monsoon rains bring relief to everything and everyone the early summer sun has scorched. The monsoons also help me track time.

I've learned that here, summer is never an endless sweaty expanse that outlasts its welcome, growing hotter and losing its magic by the day. Instead, it comes in phases that are familiar and comforting. When I see wildflowers wilting, I know there are more to come. The earth is hot to the touch and the garden is stunted, but not for long. In late summer, the monsoon season darkens an open and bright sky to drop what feels like literal buckets of rain and hail. Dry rivers and arroyos gush and flood our main streets, and my cell phone buzzes with local hazard warnings. When we are lucky enough to receive storms that temporarily patch our perpetual drought, the world is much greener, temperaments less irritable. Usually, though, the monsoon rains are too short to transform desert climates, and after a week or so, the land and everyone that depends on it returns to baking in, or hiding from, the sun.

But in the summer of 2021, my sixth year in New Mexico, the monsoon rains held on longer than I had experienced before. The shrubland around Zuni greened as expected, and this time the soil retained moisture.

Then, seemingly overnight, the lakebed swelled with water.

Water submerged the thorny weeds that had congregated at the reservoir's low points and expanded the nothing-pond into what the community began to comfortably call a lake. The K'yawaina Trail, a five-mile service road that cuts across the dam's mass, bloomed.

The dam remained a quiet and befuddling presence—unable to satisfy the hopes and dreams of the past—but it also changed, through its lake, into something novel and constantly changing.

The rain lasted long enough for me to get comfortable feeling sticky with sweat, dust, and rainfall. And instead of exclusively observing the dam itself, I also watched the sky, as the increase in water attracted more users, including Great Blue Herons and American Coots. There were also young boys in cowboy boots eager to fish and rez dogs convening in the early morning to swim. Late summer

blooms flourished in red, purple, and yellow, drawing more pollina-
tors and foragers than I had seen before. Of course, it wasn't all a joy:
mosquitoes came, too.

By the time the aspen leaves turned yellow and then orange, the
water receded modestly. But at the end of the season the community
still had a lake. For a while, I used the emotionally distant meteoro-
logical term "wet year" to describe the lakebed's altered presence. I
waved it goodbye along with everyone else, hopeful, but expecting the
dam to dry out, expecting the thorns to return.

But the following year, I could no longer see bare soil from my
back window. After our last spring frost, the driest part of the land
behind the dam—the open embankment—bloomed with acres of yellow sunflowers and plains coreopsis. Native seeds had been sheltering
underground all along, dormant, parched, and unable to fight past the
crowds of dock and cocklebur. The water gave them a boost—and
now it was their chance to dominate the landscape. I thought back to
how the air had felt still and dead during my first walk here. This time,
the air buzzed with honeybees, dragonflies, and ladybugs. Monsoons
came again in summer 2022, and the lake expanded again. The streets
flooded and previously dried arroyos bubbled with fresh water, the
dam changed again. By the next year "Top Lake" was back, and word
got out quick that there was good fishing.

Suddenly canoes and paddle boats appeared on the lake and dozens of trucks loaded with fishing gear filled its banks. Once quiet and
still, Black Rock Dam and the surrounding area buzzed with anglers
and families excited to see water. I chatted with folks on my morning
walk who told me about a guy who caught ten fish, and I listened to
jokes about the new community pool. I was rarely alone on the dam
anymore. A little water is all it took. The influx of vibrant energy from
community members made the dam less eerie and desolate. Over time,
the dam lapsed into something more like what it used to be. Or more
accurately, it entered a new phase of being while still carrying the
memory and history of the past.

My original curiosity came from a strong feeling that Black Rock Dam was both a part of and separate from the Pueblo. Both a trespasser and an obedient guest. This contradiction felt awkward and refused to settle neatly into a genuine truth about life here in Blackrock and on the dam itself. The dry embankment that eventually rebirthed Top Lake, an important appendage to the dam infrastructure, demonstrates that these static categories don't fit on a living landscape. Stubborn concrete yields to its surroundings and is placed in a state of transformation and change under pressure of the unique environment, community, and history in this place. For an idyllic desert summer, the dam held water and the people made it a hopeful vessel. The pueblo will keep this memory as the lake inevitably dries some season in the future. The dam remains but will never be quite the same.

What Emerges
on the Other Side

by
Chris La Tray

I am already quiet and reflective on a deliciously warm and sunny day in late June when the moan of the horn swells across the rolling green surface of the Blackfoot River. Not an air horn, or any other kind of human-made instrument. This is the sound of breath—from the lungs of a tall, slender guide, rising from her seat at the back of her boat, uncertain that anyone will be able to hear her—exhaled through and amplified by a large, smooth conch shell, pale and whirled with shades of brown and yellow. The note delivers a call to stillness to the rafts and kayaks and the dozen-or-so inhabitants that comprise our little flotilla. The sound is expected; what is not is how much it feels like a call to prayer. A tingle shivers up my spine.

The three other people bouncing along in the blue rubber NRS raft fall quiet with me. This is all to plan, that we will spend some of our final time together in silence. Or at least not inflict our noise onto the world. And for ten minutes, it is quiet—no sound but the breeze in the willows and ponderosas and Douglas firs crowding the river's bank, and the lapping of the water against the sides of the raft. Then the horn moans again, and we all breathe sighs of appreciation. Shortly we move alongside and below a stretch of Johnsrud Road under renovation; dust clouds the air and heavy machinery grinds and whines, announcing our arrival back into civilization. Minutes later we angle to the takeout, where we drag our rafts onto the hot sand and begin the

35

bustling process of breaking down, washing, and loading them onto trailers. Our journey together is over but for a short bus ride back to Missoula.

Nine days before our trip, on June 10, 2022, a deluge began in the Greater Yellowstone Ecosystem that lasted three days and dumped upwards of three inches of rain on the region. This event—an "atmospheric river" as it is called—followed an unusually cool and wet spring. The rain, combined with warm temperatures, unleashed epic flooding on Yellowstone National Park and its surrounding communities. The park was entirely shut down and the north entrance town of Gardiner was cut off from the rest of the world by erosion and rockslides on Highway 89, the only route into—or out of—the area. The epic devastation wrought by the rains and subsequent floods generated attention international in scope.

For all my concerns for my friends and relatives in the afflicted region, my eyes were on the Blackfoot River. Some two hundred miles north and west of the Yellowstone River, we were experiencing recent heavy rains too, and the Blackfoot was surging. The epic drama unfolding on the Yellowstone—collapsed roads and houses bobbing in the swirling brown water of the river—stirred my anxieties to a boil. I was slated to lead a writing workshop on the Blackfoot—a storied spring-and-snow-fed river that begins near the western Montana town of Lincoln and flows nearly 130 miles to merge into the Clark Fork River just outside of Missoula, near where I live—as part of an expedition with the Freeflow Institute, a Missoula-based nonprofit that mixes river trips with writing workshops.

I am of the "working writer" designation. The looming trip would be my third, but the first in inclement weather.

These workshops don't necessarily attract a crowd of dirtbag nature worshipers or river rats. Yes, there are always a couple of those folks. It's no stretch to suggest that most of us emerge from either demographic to one degree or another. Most of us are engaged in a constant struggle to cobble together a living with the things we love most: being outdoors and writing about it. We tend to gravitate toward each other. But the workshops also attract folks who have never spent much time on rivers, or even outside at all. That is the true beauty of these opportunities, but also one of the reasons I was freaking out a little.

As "the writer," I really don't have many responsibilities related to the details of pulling the trip off, but people signed up because my name is involved, and I take their safety seriously. How could I not? The best people to be with on an expedition like this are ones you can count on to have your back no matter what. But you never know about someone you don't know until you are out in it with them, do you? Unfamiliar with the people who would participate in this rainy, high-water trip, I was about to find out, for better or worse, what they were made of.

Late morning on our day of departure, a wan sunlight was making its way through the cloud cover as we gathered at the put-in to begin our adventure. Four of the five guides and facilitators involved in our trip had just been on the river the week before, arguably in worse conditions. Yes, they'd been cold, but were no worse for the wear. We stood in a small group off to the side, discussing how things might go. They assured me all would be well. We divided up the participants into rafts and a pair of inflatable kayaks and pushed off. I was relieved that the two people in the kayaks—and a third in a kayak of his own—were experienced. That was my biggest worry; I'd spent the better part of two very hot days the previous year bouncing along in one of those kayaks—"duckies" we call them—and had taken swims in the drink once or twice navigating busier water. This water was all busy and significantly burlier.

Once on the river my anxieties relaxed. The view from just above the water's surface, in a sturdy boat guided by experienced hands, is less frightening than the one from inside a car on the highway above. From that upper vantage the river appears wild and uncontrollable, bulging and splashing, entire trees propelled downriver like torpedoes.

From a boat it is more intimate, certainly not a taming, or any kind of conquering, but an interaction of ebb and flow with the immediate surroundings. We are mindful of what lies ahead, but acting only in the moment, then the next and the next, fully aware in each of them. Thrilling in larger stretches of chop and rapid, the experience is still more calming than not. It is a meditation. At least to me. Then again it could have been because Abby, the woman at the oars of the boat I was in, rowed with such calm and confidence while also participating in conversation with the rest of us that I was immediately put to ease. I chose to be in her boat for the entire trip.

The higher water leveled off some of the more turbulent stretches and rapids on this span of the Blackfoot. The speedy current also made for shorter river days, especially the first. It wasn't intended to be overly long to begin with, given our need to bus over an hour to the put-in, rig the boats, go over safety measures one more time, then push off—but not quite so short as it turned out to be. We were at our first campsite in less than an hour, if measured terrestrially, a distance of five-or-six miles or so. Measured traditionally, as by my voyageur ancestors, who paddled the rambunctious river highways of the North in heroic fashion by "pipes"—as in the number of times they could smoke through a bowl of tobacco between campsites—I suspect it was less than one or two.

Arrived, we dragged our boats onto the shore and secured them. Then we unloaded the gear, pitched our tents, set up a canopy, and settled in for an afternoon and evening of workshopping. The skies were thickly overcast but while there were occasional spits of rain, the deluge held off. That would come later and it would be apparent that the river would not be the issue; water from the sky, and the chill wind that propelled it, would present our greatest challenge.

Prayer is a loaded word. For many of us it echoes the trauma of orga-nized religion. But I have embraced the word, or an idea of it, for what it means to me. To say in English what I mean as an Anishinaabe person: I seek to live a life where every footstep becomes a prayer. This means making an effort to pray frequently, especially when undertaking anything particularly meaningful. So when we began the trip standing in the eddy of the put-in, I passed around my little bag of tobacco so that each of us might make an offering to the river. This is important; these offerings, a ritual in showing respect to the spirit of the river, are also prayers. Prayers for good weather. For safe passage. Prayers to the spirits that inhabit the world we share are necessary, if for no other reason than to show proper respect for the sheer magnificence we have, the gift we have, of being alive in a world where everything around us is alive and paying attention, too.

We are made of water. We all emerge from breath. In Anishinaabe worldview, all people result from the moment when our Creator, our Great Mystery, Kitchi Manitou, took a handful of soil from each of the four directions on Mother Earth and placed it in a shell, then breathed through it. What emerged on the other side was the first person, formed entirely of the stuff of soil and water . . . for what is breath, if not water? It flows in us. Fills us. We cannot live without it. It is something we must have every day, and what is more sacred than this?

Many of us who feel compelled to commune with wild water on a regular basis or risk detachment from the better elements of ourselves already understand this, even if we can't always articulate it very well. Rivers, creeks, streams, lakes, even rain plummeting from the heavens. Such exhilaration! The hearts that surge considering this are in the breasts of my people, the choir I sing to.

I especially love to sing these praises to others, too. I love the interactions with people outside of the usual circle, and being with them in this, for lack of a better word, ministry. The ministry of the wild, which I have little to do with. I am the doorman, really, the usher. I am not the one who exhales them full of spirit. It is the river, and the open spaces, and the trees. Maybe it is an experience they've never had before, being on the water. Maybe it is the doing of things they never expected. Like setting up and sleeping in their own tent. Or facing the up-close-and-personal relationship with the natural world without intervening walls and windows. It could even just be the challenge of sharing a communal plastic tub for shitting in. Perched there—the tub, or "groover" as it is called, situated by a conscientious guide whenever possible with a gorgeous view of the river—you have a chance, once or twice a day, to reflect alone on just where you've found yourself. Your peaceful moment might even be impeded on by other river travelers passing by. With nowhere to hide, you might as well just smile and wave. They will almost always smile and wave back.

How do we make more people care for the world like so many of us river people do? We put their butts in a boat and launch them out into it. I am convinced most people who even consider the idea will emerge from the experience changed or, more precisely, renewed into a wilder, more essentials-based version of themselves. I've seen it too often to believe otherwise.

I have a photograph of our group of writers beneath the tarp at our first campsite that first afternoon. The wind had picked up, and with it came steady rain. In the image our heads are bent over our notebooks as we scribble away, and we are bundled up as if the event were taking place in October, not June. The gloom settled in with vigor after dinner and there was little socializing—most of us just wanted to huddle warm in our tents and hope for a more pleasant morning.

I prefer not to sleep in a tent on these outings; I threw my pad and sleeping bag down on the ground under the tarp in the middle of a circle of camp chairs while everyone else sought their own sleeping shelters. The rain continued through the night. I was completely comfortable and dry, though at times the wind surged and sent spray against my face. I loved it, and the steady drum of rain on the nylon above me, even though I wondered if the collected pockets of rain might collapse my shelter.

The next morning, we packed our wet stuff and returned to the river. This would be our longest day of paddling, and it was the foulest stretch of weather, too. Waves of river water splashed up over the bow of our boats as we traversed boisterous stretches. We plunged and rose and plunged again, and the gusts of wind drove rain sharply into our faces. We were constantly wet, but our spirits remained high because it was also fun. Incredibly fun, and wondrous. During milder stretches, when the water was relatively calm and the rain abated, we talked about our life experiences, identified plants and birds, and bonded over the shared wonder of being.

We also faced reminders that this environment, for all the joy we were managing to find, could still be deadly. Hypothermia was not out of the question. I realized that when we stopped for lunch. I was perfectly warm under my rain jacket but when we secured and unloaded a few things from the boats and I unclasped my PFD, all the heat it was holding tight against my core blew away despite my fleece pullover. I began to shiver almost uncontrollably, and it was all I could do to still myself with my breath. Others were experiencing the same sensation. Our Freeflow facilitators, Kitty and Miranda, kept us busy with silly games and dances and various other flailings and cavortings while the guides threw sandwich fixings out on a table. These shenanigans not only kept us warm but they kept us laughing and in good humor, too. Then we were back out on the water for the final stretch of our day's paddle.

A couple hours later we repeated our routine of beaching, securing, and unloading the boats. This group effort multiple times a day became another ritual of bonding for our little community, because it was always all-hands-on-deck to get the tasks completed. As the shivers and chills set in again, Shredder, our lead guide, all but sprinted up the small hill to the camping area to get a fire going in his portable fire pan. Fire, blessed fire. The skies were gray, but the rain had stopped; we huddled around the flames while the guides got dinner going. The forecast for the next day hinted at better conditions, and we were hopeful; our itinerary was such that we would be at this campsite for the entire next day.

The next morning the sun arrived over the ridge to the east to hold the world in a warm embrace. Coincidentally, the arriving day happened to be the Summer Solstice. Clouds scattered and we turned our faces toward the light spreading against that wide field of gorgeous blue. The temperature rose over thirty degrees from the previous day. We hung wet gear and clothing from lush green limbs and bushes, where they steamed in the flexing warmth. Layers came off and soon our campsite was occupied by sun worshipers in shorts and tank tops. We moved our chairs out from under the sheltering tarp and formed a circle in a sandy open space with the fire tray in the middle. We gathered to eat, discuss, socialize, and write. I spent a glorious couple of hours in the mid-afternoon napping on top of my sleeping gear beneath a stand of ponderosas. As Solstice celebrations go, it is hard to imagine anyone ever engaging in one as fervently as our intrepid little river gang did. For our final writing session before dinner (is there anything better than a riverside taco bar?) the entire group turned out, guides and all. It was a special ninety minutes of sharing thoughts and stories that solidified our bonds. I didn't have to urge or even facilitate much of the interaction. It just happened, and I was grateful.

I believe there is a reason this camaraderie blossomed the way it did that afternoon, this love for each other. The word for bald eagle in Ojibwe—or Anishinaabemowin, specifically—is migizi. And sometimes migizi is simply migizi, a nonhuman relative making their way in the world just like any one of us. But sometimes they are Migizi: a guide, a spirit, or manitou. As Migizi, they represent love. And Migizi spent a large part of the afternoon with us, perched on a snag just above the clearing where we had arranged our gathering place, our place of ceremony. They were there to encourage and celebrate us. I have another photo from the trip of some of our group watching Migizi. I positioned myself to the side so that my subjects in the image are viewed in profile. Everyone is smiling, some peering through binoculars, at our spirit visitor.

Migizi was still there when I took to my nest for my nap—and gone when I woke. Shortly after, we had that final gathering, then dinner, then conversation around the fire into the night. The next day would be our last together; another short paddle, then the ten minutes of silence, of prayer, and then it would be over.

Emerging back into the day-to-day after such an experience is always a kind of culture shock. I feel the river physically moving in me for a few days more, then that too passes. The memories linger. I can still feel that rolling, waterborne sensation.

Everything in the world that spoke to our ancestors is still out there, whispering to us, hoping we will begin to listen again. Begin to pay more attention again. It is through experiences with water and trees and animal messengers that we are most likely to hear them.

I am an evangelist for water. For breath breathed through shells, and what emerges on the other side.

Lightweight

by
Daniel Rothberg

On a cool winter day, I walk to the edge of the indoor swimming pool, to a row of curved red bricks resting within the crooked imprint of my toes. I close my eyes, and then open them to an impossibly pure depth of water. Unlike the ocean or a river, everything here is visible, still.

I walk to the steps and get in. One foot, then two legs, then an entire body.

I am awoken by the presence of water around me.

My mind, so tethered to the heavy weight of an unhinged and often clumsy world, feels light. I swim through the cold waters, one stroke after another. It takes work. It's not easy even to just paddle in place. Then another stroke and another, my heart pounding with all the mechanical force necessary to carve a line. Few things, other than water, are so buoyant and heavy at once.

There was a time when I wouldn't have considered what it means to build a swimming pool in the American West. But today, when I think about an indoor pool, turn on a kitchen faucet or pass by a sprawling front lawn, I think of sitting along the Truckee River, the likely source of each chlorinated pool lane and each irrigated lawn.

The Truckee is hardly the most discussed or well-known river in the West. It's little, a narrow slip of ribbon with tributaries that rise above Lake Tahoe and—diversion after diversion after diversion—

45

descend to Pyramid Lake, the remnant of Lake Lahontan, a sea covering much of the Great Basin in the Pleistocene Epoch that ended twelve thousand years ago, a blip in geologic time.

Yet it's the Truckee's relative smallness that captured my imagination when I first moved to Reno for a job as an environmental reporter five years ago. In the hottest days of the summer, I'd go there to read and think and wander. The sound of the water would pull me from my book, each molecule gushing away downstream, almost at an instant of time, as a new collection of molecules replenished through the river, breaking over shallow rocks. Over and over again. A rhythm so integral to our existence that we are tuned to make note of it, to ask questions of it.

I'm from Southern California, where water is as illusory as the Hollywood films that helped fuel its growth. Los Angeles, a city by the sea, imports much of its water from the Colorado River, the eastern Sierra, and the State Water Project (the latter two having tentacles so far that parts of these water projects are closer to Reno than Los Angeles, cities roughly four hundred miles apart).

I grew up surrounded by the Pacific Ocean. Its waters, framed by sharp cliffs and scrub-chaparral of the coastal lowlands, seemed infinite. Water to the horizon, bobbing up and down, moving in and out. As a kid looking out at the open sea, it was hard to fathom a need for more water, even as my mom cautioned conservation.

But the city is full of signals. The mountains are mostly snowless and creeks intermittent—no match for the city's thirst for sprawling growth. And the Los Angeles River was long ago turned into a concrete ditch; without a major flood, it sits as an industrial canal, brutal and disclaimed.

Water instead comes out of the taps thanks to a neat trick of invisible pipelines, engineering that moves heavy droplets across the region, with each cubic foot gushing in at a heavy sixty-four pounds.

Water's weight doesn't change according to its location. A cubic foot weighs the same in Reno as in Los Angeles. And yet, as I sat each hot afternoon under shaded trees along the Truckee—my toes dipped in water collecting around the rocky banks—the river coursed over my feet with an airy lightness, as though it weighed nothing. The sound, a relief. The feeling, a restoration.

How could something so light weigh so much?

As my first summer living near the Truckee River turned into two and then five, I became increasingly immersed in writing about water—asking questions of where water goes and how we all relate to it. Water is the connective tissue for any ecosystem, and yet we often miss this reality in our daily lives. We do not see the snow run off and melt into creeks; this happens in a piecemeal way over time. We rarely see the pipes diverting water away from the river, or the consequences of those actions in their totality. We do not see how removing water and reengineering a stream can slice away at the species who have lived there for centuries, species like the Lahontan cutthroat trout whose evolutionary history traces back millions of years. We do not see water through the eyes of a trout or a beaver or an osprey. Nor do we witness evapotranspiration, water's journey through the roots of plants and back into the sky.

We are, in this way, blind to water, our sensory scope overloaded and still so limited.

We even freeze water to just one moment in time. Sitting beneath willows or near the wild Woods' rose, my toes touching the damp bank along the Truckee River, I can catch a water molecule in only one flash-second. Within the single blink of an eye, each molecule has slipped downstream to another point that I can conceptualize but cannot see. There is a beauty to this—the same beauty, burden, and freedom in acknowledging that no second of time can be frozen. It is an invitation to do active work, to ask questions, and to understand how a part makes a whole. No stretch of a watershed is disconnected from its other reaches, even when much of its flows are diverted. One molecule affects all others.

As a journalist, it's my job to connect the disconnected. As I started to learn more about where the Truckee flowed past and present, I started to re-interrogate the watershed where I was born.

When I was a kid, we took road trips to the eastern Sierra, where Los Angeles Department of Water and Power trucks roamed the streets of Lone Pine, Independence, and Bishop. When people spoke of Los Angeles, they did so with deep pain, a heaviness, and caution.

In the early 1900s, what was then called the US Reclamation Service played a hand in the early efforts by Southern California leaders to build the LA Aqueduct from Owens Valley. Turned on in 1913, the 223-mile aqueduct exported water from the Owens Valley, which straddles US 395, to slake the thirst of an ambitious Los Angeles. A century later, dust billowed off a desolate lake that had all but dried. And when I looked hard enough out the car window as a kid, I glimpsed the infrastructure, LADWP signs, and snaking rights of way that left this terminal lake dry.

In my 20s, when I drove down US 395 in the other direction, road tripping from Reno to Los Angeles, I started recognizing the heaviness of a system that had always been embedded deep in my life—that I had taken for granted in swimming pools, in water fountains and in lawns.

Both the Truckee River and the Owens River drain off the eastern Sierra and into the Great Basin, a land defined by water scarcity and a place where freshwater does not drain into the ocean. These two rivers pool into uncanny terminal lakes, each an oasis in the desert, a stop for shorebirds on the Pacific Flyway, and a place to recreate—a place that proves how much light a little water can bring for so many different creatures.

The Truckee River, at first glance, seems intact compared to the concrete creeks that weave through Los Angeles traffic. But few rivers in the West flow without a diversion or a dam, and for more than a century, people have manipulated the Truckee, redirecting its waters from termini that once made-up Lake Lahontan—cultural centers for the Pyramid Lake Paiute Tribe—to growing urban communities and arid farmlands.

Indeed, the Truckee is home to the first project designed under the Reclamation Act, the federal government's policy to impound rivers across the Western US, to "reclaim" a natural system for the desires of cities, farms, and homesteaders. Extractive industries and funders with pockets of East Coast capital were undeterred by the reality of the climate awaiting them, a unique aridity.

Early "reclamation" officials, including the Army Corps of Engineers, tampered with rivers all across the West. On the Truckee, the Colorado, and scores of other rivers—many of them in California—they built thousands of dams, passed new laws, and engineered new ways to tame and stretch out water supplies, untethering rivers from their ecosystems and Tribal communities who had lived alongside them since time immemorial. After breaking ground on the Newlands Project, the US Reclamation Service diverted water away from the Truckee's natural terminus at Pyramid Lake—another spiritual center for the Pyramid Lake Paiute Tribe—and directed it toward the desert town of Fallon, contributing to the delisting of a wildlife refuge at Winnemucca Lake in 1962.

I still love sitting near the wild roses along the Truckee on a raw summer day. Its shade still cools me, and I feel no less wonder as its riffles absorb the sunset's gaze. But the more I learn about the history of how this river has changed, about where the river has been and where its future might lead, my joy feels blunted. The river becomes tinged with a degree of sadness, a weight of collective loss.

For nearly two-thirds of my life, growing up in California and then living in Nevada, the West has experienced some form of drought, what scientists describe as the most extreme in 1,200 years. My mother constantly reminded us of it, urging us to take short showers. Yet no one around me, my family included, fully changed our behavior. Lawns are still ubiquitous. During the drought, some parts of LA's landscape still look impossibly palatial. In a busy, irrigated world, we all live within the individual moment, rarely conscious of what's happening upstream or aware of how we keep changing the course of rivers and remaking entire histories.

And while I understood from my mother that *we are in a drought*, the specifics can be hard to grasp, especially since the water travels from so far away. Few maps of Los Angeles include the Owens Valley, the Sacramento-San Joaquin River Delta, the Feather River, or the Colorado River, all of which feed the city's taps. Few textbooks include photographs of the headwaters for the city by the ocean or stories of what it means for an ecosystem when we dam its river and redirect its flow.

Millions of people, my family included, live in Los Angeles only because these projects exist. And it's important to note that cities like LA have made large strides in conservation, imposing watering restrictions, investing in recycling and relying more on local water supplies. But the imported water continues flowing, and it is imbued with an invisible weight.

An acre-foot of water—the standard measure water managers and farmers use, meaning the amount needed to flood an acre of land to a depth of one foot—weighs in at about 2.7 million pounds.

The physical weight of water, alone, is daunting, yet water's heaviness is built from so much more—something much lighter and less material. What does each water molecule *really* hold? It is no coincidence much of my reporting on water forces me to revisit the past. Not only are the legalities of water wrapped up in historical decisions, so too is the way water now pulses through our lives and through all of our pasts, flowing like a river to our presents and our futures.

On a recent visit to Los Angeles, I make it a point to go to the ocean, and to stop there alone, something I find myself doing more often whenever I go back to visit with family and friends.

The boardwalk bustles without any sense of organization. A woman skates by with a stroller and a barefoot man wearing tight jeans saunters between the bike path and the precipice of the sandy beach. An elderly couple, their faces worn but still luminous, hold hands and gaze out at the sea.

When I was younger, I always enjoyed the energy and constant movement of a beach separating city and ocean. No matter how hard one tried, no one could take up too much space.

Today, it's a warm Saturday at the cusp of my favorite season, spring, a transitory time that defies any label in Southern California. I take off my running shoes and walk on the sand, letting the grains sift through my toes, feeling the heaviness and effort required to walk through what alone are the miniscule flakes from rocks.

I walk and walk, and walk into the sea, cold and refreshing.

Few things underscore the awesome, untamed heaviness and lightness of water like ocean waves. I remember all the times growing up, when I had been laundered through them, pushed down and spun over, feeling scared and exhilarated, as though I might be stuck there forever.

Perhaps water is both heavy and light, something that shifts in shape and in memory—flowing through time and formed by its passage—something so essential it does not exist on any binary.

I watch the sea pull its weight inward, collecting its heaviness to make a wave. It curves near the flat shore and snaps with the same joyful noise as the tail of a humpback whale. I step further and let the water percolate before I dunk my body in the sea. It is still buoyant, and heavy, all at once.

by
Sarah Gilman

Terra Affirma

Water eats, Earth drinks

It is impossible to name all the ways
that water finds to go underground.

On the Kaibab Plateau, on the north rim
of the Grand Canyon, it's a miracle
that it does at all.

A mere 30 inches of precipitation
fall on its summit per year, and
16 on its flanks, but the air
is dry enough to evaporate
two to four times that.

No perennial streams flow
across the Kaibab's surface.

Its water comes
in pulses:

snowmelt in spring,
the flooding pound
of monsoon thunderstorms
in late summer.

This water quickly filters down
through sinkholes,
fractures, and faults,
then settles into
layers
of
Sandstone
and limestone
left by an
ancient
sea.

Water has an appetite, and here it gorges, hollowing out

Corridors and caves

and pits and tubes.

After thousands of feet of descent, and dozens of miles of traverse, streams and rivers born in the dark break free and tumble from the Grand Canyon's walls.

Once, an author friend climbed into the rushing mouth of the largest of these falls, hundreds of feet up a cliff. He and his companion wedged their way through tunnels and swam wide caverns for a quarter mile until the chill turned them back.

Later, he wrote that he remembered the silence of the spring's deeper chambers most of all.

It felt like the beginning of the world.

And it was, in a way:
Earth meets water's hunger
    with its own thirst—gulping
its gaps and cracks full,
    carving the strata of its
        oldest memories into
            something new.

        Sometimes,
    it swallows
whole rivers.

In Slovenia,
the Reka disappears
into an intricate
cave system
for 24
miles
before
surfacing
in Italy
as the
Timavo.

The Santa Fe
does the same
for three miles
in Florida.

The Mojave,
in California, can seem
more like a ghost
than a river,
Flowing beneath its bed
through the sand.

That's how it is
with the Methow
in Washington, where
I live—whole stretches
moving out of sight
through glacial debris
during dry late summer
and deepest winter,
when our moisture
mostly falls
as snow.

When I catch
those snowflakes
in my mouth,
their melt   water
makes my   throat
a subterranean   creek,
feeds countless   tributaries,
fans through   every delta
in my flesh   until
it is as   saturated
                   as soil
                   after
                   a long
                   storm.

I once
visited the same
Grand Canyon falls
that my friend
climbed inside.

The river plunged
from a sheer
rockface down
a series
of terraces.

We stripped
and
stood beneath.
The falls hit
my shoulders
like a slap:
the sound of

water colliding
with water through
a tight drum
of living skin.

—Sarah
Gilman

The Undertow

by
Laura Paskus

*F*or all but four (potentially glorious, perhaps just unexcavated) years of my life, I've been qualmish around water—hypervigilant of rivers and lakes, riptides and waves, water in roadways, and mud that slicks tires into uselessness.

I'd long blamed my father, who incessantly warned my brother and me away from fast rivers, polluted bays, bottomless quarry lakes, sucking shorelines, and quicksandy pond bottoms. Who kept a pipe wrench in the basement and cranked off the water if anyone showered in summer for more than a few quick strokes with soap and shampoo. (Banging on the door allowed bathers too much autonomy. Better to keep them anxious and therefore efficient.)

I still wade into the ocean, swim sloppy strokes in the lake, kayak the river. But I am weird and watchful and wary in a way that embarrasses me.

And tucked inside my consciousness is the story of a memory, or the memory of a story.

It starts with delight. With toes and heels, arches and calves in water white with bubbles. It starts with smooth sand, a gray and undulating Atlantic. Holding my mother's hand at first, then pulling free. Captivated, as hissing sands cover my feet. Then, a parting from sand and from sky as the undertow pulls me under the waves. Gasps and salt and a stranger's chest, and from there a slide into a viscous story my mother has half-told a half-dozen times of seeing her child pulled into, then from the ocean.

My mother, I should note, is an unreliable narrator. As kids, my brother and I used to laugh about her memory. Now I understand: she reframes the world to make it manageable and malleable.

While I doubt the details of the story, scant and rote as they are, muscle memory murmurs that the undertow's grip was honest. I've never failed to understand that waters feel desire, and to wonder if someday they'll be back for me.

As soon as I understand it's an option, I leave for the desert.

Just out of college, I'm hired onto a crew excavating pre-Pueblo sites that will be destroyed when the road is widened through Coyote Canyon on the Navajo Nation. The summer's monsoon storms arrive at the exact same time; the boss says I carried water with me from the East Coast. Though intoxicated by the waves of thunder barreling across the landscape—and thankful for rain's relief on afternoons buzzing with heat—I don't yet understand everyone's mania for rain dropping from the sky. But within a few years of living here, and then as drought grips the Western US, I dread the crank of the pipe wrench.

Soon, the rivers dry.

Starting around the early 2000s, the Pecos River and the Middle Rio Grande dry almost every summer when irrigation districts divert all the waters for fields and orchards, leaving mud and then sand for fish and beavers, cottonwood copses and groundwater tentacles, herons and coyotes, and house finches that should sing through the morning. By the summer of 2022, the Rio Grande dries for an even simpler reason: there isn't enough water in upstream reservoirs.

For decades as a journalist, I obsessively cover rivers, groundwater, wildfire, and climate change. I report the data, the endless facts; I interview scientists and elders, excavate the histories of water wars, and share news of the wildlife who suffer when rivers and springs and meadows start to shrink. I hike up channels full of gasping or rotting fish, press my fingers into the prints of coyotes and raccoons who feast before starving, listen to the aching quiet when the summer birds have nothing to sing for, when the swallows disappear because there aren't insects to eat.

Always, I need to know where the waters go, what happens when they disappear. There's more to the straightforward story I untangle for readers, reciting for them facts about interstate water compacts and infrastructure and greenhouse gas emissions. There's more to the story, if I'm honest about what I feel and about what I've witnessed.

As it has warmed, the world here has become drier, and everything is thirstier, including forests, orchards, farmlands, and the air conditioners we crank up as heat waves deepen and expand. Without ceremony, the waters who dwelled in our rivers and springs and reservoirs started sneaking away—finding other ways to live, without us and beyond our neglect.

Driving to Santa Fe on a mad cloudy Thursday with my daughter, we cross the Rio Galisteo, a now-ephemeral tributary of the Rio Grande that cuts out of the Sangre de Cristo Mountains. The dry arroyo stretches toward Kewa Pueblo in the late afternoon light, dusty and bright.

Later, on our return to Albuquerque, with a black and rippling cloud parked atop the Sandia Mountains and a slice of tangerine sky hanging on in the west, we cross the riverbed again. This time, water's silver figure flows in S's across the sands, snaking through the arroyo under the cover of twilight's descent, not wanting to be seen.

At home in the shower, I whisper to water: Where do you come from? What do you know? The water gurgles back—stories of falling from clouds to high headwaters and dripping past tongues into bowels—then slides off my body and down the drain into darkness. I want to be a better vessel, a holy conduit. I want to remember how to carry her, how to live fully and freely within her embrace. I want to know how to tell true stories about her.

She Wants to Be a River

by
Michelle Otero

*T*hat summer he turned five, each time it rained, my stepson would ask, "Is the drought over?" We found different ways of telling him it would take more—so much more—to pull New Mexico out of megadrought.

This is the last summer he will live with us. I can already feel him pulling away. He chose a college in the Pacific Northwest. The school has Vitamin D lamps for students from sunny climates.

His older sister walks the bosque most evenings after working all day at a horse farm. The animals calm her. With horses she is present, patient. She is capable. After work she is restless. The used Honda we bought her before this job, before the winter, before that morning she called for help, sits unused in the driveway. The front bumper is held by painter's tape. The rims that came with the vehicle are long gone, one perhaps on a curb near an ex-boyfriend's house, one in a tow yard, one in the trunk, another in a landfill. Most evenings she perches on a fallen cottonwood jutting into the Río Grande.

They called it their tree when they were small. We would walk the acequias from our house to the river. Sometimes we might pack a lunch. Winters, the kids would scramble into the dry ditches and walk below us, their own hidden path. Of course, we could always see them. Of course, they knew that. Sometimes our dogs would join them. Once we reached the river, one dog would drink, the other would stay with us grownups on dry land.

61

This spring and summer, snowmelt from Colorado and northern New Mexico carves new streams into the bosque. We douse ourselves in mosquito repellent. My stepdaughter scratches every bite, turning each prick into a bloody welt. A co-worker at the horse farm asks if she fights, if that's why her legs and arms are covered in scabs and scars.

I am grateful for every drop of rain. I welcome cloudy days, but only one at a time, and only with at least one week's distance in between.

I am from light, from sun and warmth, from Deming, New Mexico, thirty miles north of the US-Mexico border, a place hotter and drier than the Albuquerque's South Valley, where I've lived since my downtown apartment was destroyed in a fire and I moved in with my now husband and now stepkids fourteen years ago.

Like my stepson, I also pulled away from the people I loved that summer before I left home for college. Like him, I chose a place far from the one that raised me, a place more than a thousand miles from home, a place near water. My grade point average was higher than his, but he is better prepared, more curious, less defensive, more aware of what he doesn't know. I still carry eighteen-year-old me in her waffle knit JC Penney thermals, cracking a window because she can't control the knocking radiator, worried one of the stalactite icicles hanging from the eaves of every dorm, every lecture hall, every building might fall and impale her as she walks to her library job. His winters will be less severe, but every bit as gray. Will he ask for help? Will he sit under the Vitamin D lamps? Will he want to come home?

Since winter, there's a cloud over my house. It casts shadows but offers no water.

Drought is a girl who empties a fifth, swallows every pill, a girl drowning in her bed, winter snow everywhere but our yard, our trees, our cottonwood leaves gathered, mulched, wind-scattered. A girl trying to walk to her door and falling and falling and calling for help and falling through her brother's hands, a girl seizing on her bedroom floor.

In the emergency waiting room I stare at a bottle of Sam's Choice water left on a magazine table with no magazines. I wait wait wait.

Water is a period on my fifty-first birthday, a spot, a flood.

Drought is a birthday walked past like an unmarked gravestone. What is fifty-one when the girl in our house doesn't want to live?

How long is winter? How long is drought?

I am not Jesus. I do not walk on water. I do not want to write a dry river. I want to write a poem in sand.

The girl in our house says she wants to be a river. She wakes every morning, and she is still in this human body. She wants to be a constellation. She wants to be a star.

What have we given them?

How many times can we say in one season, *This has never happened* (pandemic), *this is unprecedented* (January 6), *it's never been this bad* (wildfires in April)?

The girl is dry and doesn't want to be. She walks the Río Grande. Drinks. She is reverse Llorona, looking for Mother.

What is my restoration? What is my salt cedar? My invasive species?

She feeds horses along the ditch with horsetail she pulls from the root. She doesn't ask the plant for permission. Horsetail stops bleeding, heals wounds.

Like my mother, my stepdaughter never learned to swim. Is this inheritance if she is not mine? Four summers ago—before emergency room, before tall boys and Jim Beam, before so many pills—she and I parasailed above the Caribbean while her dad and brother built sandcastles. The next day we visited a cenote. She wore a life jacket, navigated taut rope to buoy to ladder to dry land where she stayed as her brother leapt from rock ledge to water.

She says he is sheltered. She wonders how he will make it so far from home on his own.

I call her girl. She is young woman. Her brother is young man.

I always seem to be missing something, a box left in someone's attic, a package never arrived. I dream I'll find that bag of lace, the German shepherd mix I never brought home from the shelter, the children I forgot to have.

I once loved a man who was bad for me. He was when I started drinking coffee. We traveled to France together, visited Chartres. At the Cathedral our guide pointed to Mary in stained glass, her blues and reds as vibrant as overripe fruit.

"During World War Two the people of the village removed the glass panels one by one and stored them in cellars to protect them from German bombs."

What would my people hide in time of war? Water? A boy? A girl?

The girl in my house covers scars on her wrists, cuts her hair with a hunting knife.

She wants to be loved more than she wants to be alive. She is endangered.

A Letter from the Confluence of a Very Old River

by
Aaron A. Abeyta

*D*ear M,

Yes, all of this is sorrow. I apologize in advance. I have been writing these letters for many years now, always on some topic that seems as foreign to me as breathing under water, resilience is no different, though I struggled in the pit of my soul to tell my brain: be positive damn it, before the entire world begins to think that you live in the saddest place in the universe; tell them how your people have survived for generations, their lives held together by an ancient dialect of Spanish, Nahual, English, and even a small teaspoon of French here and there. Tell them how your abuelita would fry you an egg on winter mornings, how the puela would pop and sizzle while your young heart filled with how much you loved her. I want to tell you all of these things at great length, but, alas, I cannot.

Sometimes, in the pre-dawn we see the ghosts as they move up and down main street, malnourished doppelgangers intent on their morning bottle. There is no buoyancy in their stride, in their lives. Their failures and their pain were predicted before they were born. We can spot them, the oncoming brokenness of being that is my gente; we have become the weathermen of damaged things, able to spot the low-pressure fronts above the San Juans, the shifting jet stream of prosperity, the storm that is forming off the coast of some distant place over some ocean that most of these ghosts will never see. We name their thin and frail bodies so that our children will know them, so that they may avoid the gravity that holds them in their orbit of failure. Look, mijo, that one is a waste of God-given talent. That one is a bum. That one, mijo, he could shoot the basketball, but his name is acid now, drugs, mijo, the acid fried his brain. And that one, the one on the corner, his legs bowed like a harp placed in front of a mirror, that one was beaten with a bat. And that one, his father never loved him. And that one over there is just like his father. Yes, mijo, sometimes prison is hereditary. And that one, your classmate, try to be nice to him; his mother was driving home one night, the pass was so icy. I'm going to tell you something, mijo, our secret, please do not tell your friends; they will just make fun of him. When he drinks, which is always, he takes his mother's high school ID out of his wallet and he stares at it. Be nice to that one, mijo, I don't know why God has done that to him. And so, we name and continue to name them, their stories are our warning, and here is a small truth that makes the subject of this letter nearly impossible; I have only named a few of them.

It's an easy enough assumption. The ghosts are so visible, there on the main drag. They have been there so long we cannot know if the gutted buildings they lean up against need their thin bodies to remain standing or if the reciprocal is true. People drive through and they make the easy assumption that everyone makes when looking at broken and abandoned things. This place is poor. The assumption itself is not incorrect, but I'm going to offer that the assumption is so rarely benign or born of winged things that might make a positive difference. Poverty has always been the excuse for exploitation, the knife sharpened against the benevolent idea that help is being offered.

At the south end of town there are black railcars owned by a multi-million-dollar, multi-national company that calls itself Energy Solutions. The black gondolas wait on the tracks like tumors. They have been there over a year, patient as only nuclear gondolas can be, their hollowed bellies waiting for the cargo of nuclear waste from Los Alamos National Laboratories. To the north of the black gondolas the Rio San Antonio flowers over an ancient skull of volcanic rock, and I imagine that the rock remembers its fiery birth, holds it, cool now, a heart of pain that keeps the river flowing. You see, John, there are so many ghosts that we keep alive, all of them are passed down to us, hereditary markers where we store pain, loss, humility, humiliation, as well as the small crumb of love we keep in our vast heart of longing. It's funny. No, it's sad. Our resilience is our pain. We too, like the bed-rock of the river, were born in the shadow of an ancient volcano. Our land was stolen and then our water. Our language was next. A young boy sincerely asks me what I think of the black railcars. I tell him that I expected them all along. I mean this. Most everyone believes that they just arrived one day, and that is technically correct. They did appear without an announced warning, but we have all been instructed by our loss.

"Mijo, remember how they stole our water. It will become their habit."

So, I tell the boy, they already took the land and water, now they are coming for our health. This is the story of conquest; every geno-cide has its railcars.

As I began this letter I could not shake an image. It is still with me, and though I cannot find it on the internet I see it there in my brain, permanent as memory will allow. Primo Levi called her the Hiroshima Schoolgirl. She was one of the 150,000 vaporized, her shadow burned permanently into a wall. I find images of other shadows, a man who was waiting for a bank to open, the shadow of leaves, the shadows of handrails, but I cannot find the girl's shadow.

Los Alamos calls it "legacy waste." This is their way of say-ing that the uranium, PCBs, and radon are the byproduct of a heroic endeavor that ended the Second World War. They make it a point in the public meetings to tell us of its origins. You see the implication; it is our duty as patriots to accept what the Department of Energy sends us because this waste, this legacy waste, saved American lives. I want to remind them that more Americans died in Hiroshima and Nagasaki than in the attacks of 9/11, but that would be a futile rebuttal to their jingoistic rhetoric. They don't care about Americans, past or present. Nuclear waste is money. Plutonium pits are money. Exploratory drilling is money. The entire war complex is money. Make no mistake, it is so difficult to be resilient when every force of nature seems intent on your destruction. Nuclear has become synonymous with three things: poverty, people of color, and greed.

My wife and I have a friend named Marie Max. She is from Cameron, Arizona; she is Navajo, and she tells us how the elementary school has water fountains wrapped in cellophane, the water too dangerous to drink because the uranium the government mined has leeched into the water supply. I think of Marie often. I'm not Navajo, but she says that I remind her of a Navajo; it is one of the finest compliments I have ever received. She gives me an eagle feather after I read poetry to her. She doesn't explain why; I gladly accept. I think of Marie for many reasons, often at restaurants. I remember how she refused the bread brought to our table by a waitress at Outback Steakhouse. She made the woman take it back and bring her a loaf that didn't have the knife sticking out of it. Her point was simple. Why would you stab your food? I love to fish; it is my most basic form of peace. Current practice tells us that all anglers should release what they catch, return the fish to the river for sustainability and healthy rivers. I think of Marie Max every time I release a fish; I apologize to the animal for tormenting it solely for my pleasure. I don't know why I am telling you this. It must make sense, somewhere, somehow.

The gondolas wait for their cargo 250 feet from the river. The cargo arrives on flatbed trucks, the waste in soft-sided containers dubiously called "super sacks," glorified water-resistant tarps. They are loaded onto the gondolas by crane; any accident or spill would, within minutes if not seconds, end up in the river, the town's water supply, the lifeblood of the acequias east of town, the water that blooms our fields, waters our animals, and makes us whole.

Those ghosts, the ones I spoke of earlier. They have begun to write. They are finally asking to be heard. The town park is filled with their tags and graffiti. They announce their life in black paint. They claim this sad acre of park, where children rarely play, as their own. I believe in symbols, they have killed the park, the empty swings, the tagged slide. Their anger is palpable. Their abandonment has been complete for generations. So what is my point? Honestly, I'm not sure. I know this is all supposed to be connected. That is a writer's job, to connect what the heart knows to what the eyes see. These connections, these too are resilience, I suppose.

Energy Solutions and the railroad tell us the waste shipments will bring economic viability to Antonito. Their own documents tell us that one to three jobs will be created and that through the course of the "campaigns," one to eight deaths can be expected as well. They want to ship the waste in perpetuity. That's a fancy word for forever, but we knew that before they opened their mouths. They see our ghosts, our beaten park, the worn sidewalks of despair. They see how we take every failure, cut it open, weigh and measure the vital organs, always looking for the source, the failed motor that caused the living host to succumb to his aching life and thus conquer it by dying. They see these things and therefore view our poverty as weakness. They see our fallen things and imagine it must mean complacency and apathy. Put a different way, they believe we won't fight back.

Gerald Vizenor coined a term: Survivance. The root is simple, survive. It's almost an equation, survival + perseverance = living. Or survival + resistance, or sustenance, or defiance, or assistance, or appearance, or circumstance. Or perhaps on a lighter note, survival + dance or chance = a better life. Perhaps it is survival + resilience. I know the suffix does not quite fit, but I think the gesture is accurate, the intent is pure enough to make it true. I mentioned earlier that our resilience is our pain, but I have written myself out of that assumption, though I may come back to it once I leave your Headwaters and return to my own. Instead, I see now how our survival is our resilience. We will never bounce back to our original form as the definition of the word implies. Those days are gone, absent as a brief push of wind, here then gone. No, I suppose our survival and therefore our resilience will depend entirely on how long we wish to fight.

And what of those ghosts, those walking frailties of bone and poverty? I think of Marie Max, her refusal of the stabbed bread. I think of the town park overrun with graffiti and broken bottles. A question emerges: why? Over 225,000 people died in Hiroshima and Nagasaki. Their deaths were dropped on them with a parachute tethered to an atomic bomb. Their deaths were the result of genius minds working at evil intent. Antonito is in Colorado, but we are, culturally, linguistically, religiously, spiritually, and emotionally tied to the people and places of northern New Mexico. Those 225,000 lives disappeared in an instant of demon wind and heat, and I have heard how all the radiation entered into the sky, how the wind brought it across the Pacific. You see, John, I don't want to be too melodramatic here, but I think you can see where I'm going with this. There must have been souls on that wind too, souls looking for the source of their destruction. I'm not entirely naïve. I don't buy into a whole lot of hocus pocus, but I don't believe that northern New Mexico and southern Colorado are some of the poorest places in the country simply because they are isolated. Can you imagine the weight of 225,000 deaths, how heavily that weighs on even the potential for resilience?

I realize that this letter is getting long. Perhaps you are tired. I will not be long in finishing. This is my first letter to you, however. I have written many to your predecessor and several to this somewhat anonymous group we call The Headwaters. But since this is my first letter to you, I thought I should tell you that all is not death and poverty. I want you to know that I love my hometown. There are brief and brilliant moments of light, the sun through a kitchen window, neighbors that always wave as they pass, a herd of sheep as they emerge from the trees into a meadow, a river that forgets the sins we have committed against it, the memory of my abuelita frying me an egg on a winter morning, two kids just barely in love, holding hands as they walk down main street, a football team that takes the field one autumn and brings hope where none had previously resided. Yes, there are great storehouses of beauty, each made manifest by some small gesture or action. I want you to know that the gondolas have not moved in over a year. We are resilient enough to fight. We are in a great struggle of will and determination versus millions and millions of dollars, but we know, despite our losses, despite our ghosts, that the river is our home, that the river makes our home possible, that the river in its many moods and flows is the truest metaphor, it teaches us how to be, and at its lowest, when she appears dry and weak, we know beneath the rock of volcanoes and distant pressures, that the river still flows, invisible, subterranean, toward a confluence of hope, a place where it emerges from the earth sweet and cold, perhaps flowing into a greater river which flows toward a greater river and so on, our own resiliency borne there upon the riffles and currents, our lives complete, our ghosts smiling up at the passing earth, as the river carries them.

Much peace,
a.

The Shape of Goodbye

by
Christi Bode

*T*oday, I'm not feeling the stoke of fresh powder. I want to remind others of how fleeting it all is, how easily it can be taken away. Confronting the grief of a disappearing Winter feels more tolerable if I make other people see it, too. This feels like the metamorphosis of a complex goodbye: reluctance and heartbreak entangled with joy. I feel this messiness inside, as my body attempts to sort through my own losses in a way that my heart can comprehend. This loss is buried seven layers deep, in a place accessed only by the use of sterilized tools intended to remove the source of pain.

I stare at the monochrome canvas in front of me, searching for signs of weakness. The wind pushes loose facets across the surface, revealing a solid layer that refuses to give.

The subtle changes happening in between the folds of these mountains are cumulatively profound. Spruce trees are constantly shedding needles, fighting to stay in balance with a root system stressed from years of drought. Ponderosa pine seedlings migrate fifty feet higher, searching for better growing conditions as temperatures warm. A lack of sticky resin on the bark leaves trees more vulnerable to insect infestation. This hotter, drier climate leads to millions of acres of deadfall, meaning less canopy and more sunlight penetrating the floor.

Watching the forest struggle to find equilibrium is like holding onto a womb that can no longer support life. The vessel is there, but there is nothing to fill it with.

• • •

For now, I am hidden under layers of wool, fleece, and Gore Tex. I tug on my neck gaiter to hide the movement of my lips, for when I inevitably curse at my body for not doing what I want it to do. I pull down my goggles, which typically aren't rose-colored. In front of me is a fiercely fragile landscape that determines everything about our future.

Long Trek, Montezuma, and Square Top are familiar faces among the south San Juan Mountain range in southern Colorado. My knowledge of them has evolved from topographic lines on a map to experiencing the swells and lulls of seasons. The San Juans hold special memories: A marriage proposal on top of Bonito Pass. Spreading ashes of beloved friend in a meadow overlooking the Rio Grande. Catching my first cutthroat trout at Crater Lake. Crossing paths with a mountain lion on Del Norte Peak. Losing my car keys in La Garita Creek. Tracing the Continental Divide with the wings of a single-engine plane.

My job is to help others to understand the significance of these water towers, whether you live one or one thousand miles downstream. As an environmental filmmaker, I am always searching for a scene that reminds the audience of what's worth saving, worth remembering. I've stood on a bare tundra in the middle of January. I've seen peaks coated in white at the end of May. Archives upon archives of digital files sit on my shelf, documenting times of bounty intermittently dispersed by times of scarcity. I love these mountains through the swings, despite their appearance. I love them because they're the shape of home and they meet me where I am. Even today.

A flurry of powder hounds[1] beeline to the ski lift, eager to make first tracks[2] for the day. I strap one wobbly leg into my snowboard and use the other to push forward. A green blur passes me to the left and stops; I sign quietly, indicating I'm a single and he can join me on the

---

1   *A person who strives to grab the deepest days of the season, wherever the fresh powder may be, and have the personal mobility, freedom and financial means to do so.*
2   *Cutting through fresh snow before anyone else does, leaving your trail for all else to see.*

lift. This means I will have company for the next seven minutes and I suck at small talk. The lift makes a recognizable pattern of sound—humm humm humm, click clack click clang clang—queuing me to brace for the chair behind.

Everything feels worthy of my attention. The way a snowdrift creates a convex on the side of a cliff, or how flakes disappear into the air. Dead tree branches give way to the weight of heavy snow. I move my worried gaze from the tree, to the sky, and then the ground. Stopping, watching, wondering.

If everything demands my attention, what's left for me?

My wound has healed, but the scar tissue is tender. My heart, even more so. A thin, white line follows the curvature of my lower abdomen. It is lightly pronounced like a ski track blanketed under a couple inches of fresh powder, reminding me of who I once was. Snow fills in the old tracks with ease; my brain's weather struggles to make sense of the internal gaps between organs.

I want my ski lift companion to understand the layers of the mountains. I want him to learn the language and be willing to talk about these changes with me.

I also want the world to accept my softness, tenderness. For a long time, I have been sealing off parts of my grief, both the larger losses—like an entire ecosystem and the relatively smaller ones. The smaller ones that aren't so small, like the loss of my health and my identity and the possibility of motherhood as I had always understood it.

After a long minute, my lift companion and I launch into pleasantries: Yes, the snow is powdery. Oh, you're a local? No, I do not come here every day. I have a job. What do you do for work?

In one oxygen-deprived exhale, I tell him how ski areas are only profitable fifteen days out of the season and that this hobby has a limited shelf life. I tell him how many people and creatures are dependent on these waters and snows and pathways below our feet, and the creatures are the ones ultimately losing everything. I tell him how our kids and our kids' kids won't experience a succession of big winters, but cling onto the hope of one emerging the following year. Or maybe the year after that. That's what we always cling on to: the promise of a good winter to save us.

Seven minutes pass and this episode of *Christi Ruins Everything* comes to an end. We glide off the lift in opposite directions and a blast of cold wind throttles me back into the moment. I am at the top of the Continental Divide, where water decidedly goes east or west, left or right. Dappled light reveals mountain ranges and hides others. My lower abdomen releases a pulse of dull pain. I finally feel safe to take my mask off.

A mountain is a body of water. It has a head. Its thinking gets cloudy, then parts to clarity. Its core gives away when the weight pressing down is too heavy. It has veins and a heartbeat. It remembers everything but doesn't forgive all of the time.

I bend down to strap my other foot into the binding and lose balance. My tailbone lands first and I welp into the wind. I try to stand up and fall again. A warmth rushes to the corners of my eyes as my body releases pain. Tears hit the crystalized surface, joining the other bazillion frozen molecules that could split east or west, but will never see the ocean. It's my physical contribution to the watershed. Maybe it's a bigger contribution than any ski lift epilogue or film I could make about Her. Climate work—the act confronting an existential threat head-on—is a full body immersion.

Am I living life, as women are expected to live, with an integrity of purpose in place, if I no longer have a womb? A part of me is relieved I don't have to make a decision about bringing a child into the world at a time of ecological collapse. I won't have to show a genetic mirror of myself photos from the past and reminisce about the days where snow lasted for months instead of weeks.

But I am also angry that this choice wasn't mine to make. The single, permanent remedy meant removing organs vital to creating life, which were seriously compromising my own. I had a certain heroic expectation of how this surgery would work; it was an intervention at a critical moment in my life with a clear, calculable outcome. There were things the doctor didn't tell me about, the things you can't detect on an ultrasound or in lab tests. I will never have the chance to pass along my intimate knowing of these mountains, and what it means to love a place beyond hope. I'm trying to learn that there is something deeper than hope, deeper than what cells create in a womb: It's a language of mothering and seeing that everything has meaningful speech. Mothering is a wide-ranging act that has no biological requirement.

I imagine what these mountains will look like in one hundred years. Simplicity reigns. In remote pockets of this range, it will still be possible to experience the San Juans in their primordial state. Water, rock and vegetation will keep blending together. There will be others who attend this place with discernment, an open heart, and an attuned ear. Creating in a time of crisis looks like advocacy, communication, education, art, or action. It could mean having a child. The world needs both.

River Song

by
Santana Shorty

In the early days you sang to me.
Took my hand in your palm and patted it with the other.
Like you were making sure I was still there, reaffirming my presence.

I knew you loved me when you asked me to walk in the moonlight
    with you.
What for? I asked.
To see you, you answered.

And so we would walk along the river, its pale current shining with a
    white glow.
The owl called out, warning us of our mortal folly and fate.
A tarantula poked along, savoring the last embers of heat in the
    pavement.
An elk tiptoed down the mesa, its nose flared by the scent of water.
Two lovers walked to the river's bank, joining the other creatures
    who sipped the water and filled their bellies.

You sang me a love song in your language.
Sometimes you started a verse with *baby girl* or *my honey.*
I blushed, but you couldn't see.
Or chose not to.

It's been years now. Too many moons have passed.
I hear your singing when I walk at night in my sleep.
In my dreams I go to the river, but it is now a stream.
It is dark.
I keep walking.
Your voice echoes through the canyons, gargled, far.

The owl wakes me.
It scolds me for not listening.
I did listen, I tell it.
Just not to you.

Letter Born of a Snowy Morning

by
CMarie Fuhrman

McCall, ID
March 31, 2023

*D*ear Friend,

Today I have a mind of snow, but a heart of spring.

It seems today may be the day the sun breaks finally through the foam of clouds like a Steelhead breeching from icy depths. Yesterday, another six inches of snow fell on these Salmon River Mountains. This morning, filling the kettle, I marveled at the snow several inches up the kitchen window. I am surrounded by water and yet, do not drown. I look above the snow, to the forest beyond our cabin and try to imagine a different scene, one not dichromatic. When the limbs of pines were not heavy with snow and the transplanted rhubarb, now nearly six feet below this winter white, was leafy and green. I turn the kettle on to boil and though I know better, I think there is no way all of this snow will ever melt, can ever be gone from our woods, will never not be enough.

But the sun is writing the truth on the landscape and the birds deliver the lines to the air. This should be evidence enough, but we keep turning to other sources, sources outside ourselves and away from nature for proof. As if it can be found by a search engine, as if it needs to be spoken in our language. The lines of this morning's poem are written in a vocabulary we have forgotten, an instinct we no longer trust, an inward search rarely taken. They are written for a world yet created, known by all our ancestors, and with an intelligence we have yet to achieve.

Though Saturdays, for me, are usually filled with much of the domestic, I pushed chores aside and sat in my reading chair and watched the weather come. It was so like a spring storm! Blizzard of fine snow, then flakes the size of a squirrel's fist, then graupel, then sun. All the while the birds feasted on seeds in the feeders and then on the seeds that blew to the ground. Birds came like messages from the land's imagination. Dark-eyed Juncos, Mountain and Black-Capped Chickadees, Red-breaster Nuthatches—and the bigger birds, too—Flicker, Steller's Jays, and Downy. Despite the wind and snow and cold they sang and chattered. Maybe not despite it all, maybe it was because of it all they sang.

Funny, isn't it, how we have come to talk about the weather. Around town people are cursing the snow and the pattern of storm upon storm and the gray days they bring. They long for weather that suits their needs, whatever those may be, or perhaps they're just ready to put the heavy coats and broad shovels away. Just yesterday, while brushing the truck off for a trip to town, a neighbor pulled up next to me and said, "This fucking snow. I've had enough of it." I must tell you, I winced. His anger, though directed at the snow, felt personal. But I've been there. There is a work to winter that sometimes feels an inconvenience to our human ways, and there have been times when brushing or scraping the windshield, shoveling the driveway, or being denied a visit because of bad roads has caused me contempt toward the weather as well. But that's changing.

Last spring, I learned that in Haida culture to curse the weather is to offend the weather. How foolish not to trust something far wiser and ultimately far more powerful than humans. Like the beings with whom I share this place, I now thank the weather as well. Sometimes, I find myself apologizing, for it can be argued that we and our ways have influenced the weather now, changed or altered its behavior. This, above all, should be a stronger argument against cursing it. When Samuel L. Clemens wrote, "Everyone complains about the weather, but no one does a thing about it," he was talking about one thing, now it means something entirely different.

The snow is so deep, the neighbor's cabin can no longer be seen and the youngest pines in our mixed conifer forest are completely covered. I almost wrote "buried" instead of covered, but there is nothing dead about the scene. I like to think of the cold and white that covers the small trees is a quilt with a batting of winter that knows how to tuck a young pine in. I imagine what those saplings might feel as the snow becomes their air and sky and, when winter finally covers our kitchen window, I might know. Well, it will be an abstract knowing, as I need these walls as protection. Yet the comfort of this snow is something I think I do understand.

My partner, Caleb, calls this Salmon Weather and I have started calling the snowstorms Salmon Weather also, and the snow, Salmon Snow. I love that name; it alludes to an insurance, but also to a future I'm hoping will arrive. Here, at six thousand feet, the snow is deep and will hang around until June, but up higher, in the places where winter is a song sung even on summer mornings, the snow can hold out into July and August, like a reservoir, melting slowly, releasing water to streams, which flow into rivers. This cold runoff will come when the rivers are at their lowest, their warmest: when Salmon are returning, when most fish are spawning, when water, preferably cool water, is what these fishes need most. Another name I love: cold water refugia. What poet wouldn't love such a phrase; what mortal sinner could resist the word "refugia."

Refugium, refugia, Latin for refuge, for hideaway. The words deliver a sense of relief, elicit a memory of safety, or at least the expectation of some kind of temporary amnesty; a rest. The forest has often been my refuge, the wild places, the copse of trees or a mountain lake a shelter from the conditions of living, a safe place, too, like the arms of a good mother or accepting lover, or the deep belly fur of my old dog where I bury my face and cry for the years we've had, the months we've left. Cold water refugia is all this, but on a piscine level. In rivers, refugia can come in the form of upwellings, can flow from the mouths of streams, can exist in the shade of bankside trees. Rest areas for salmon and steelhead making the long trip home; equally necessary for aquatic dwellers seeking relief from rising river temperatures.

It's arduous enough, the nearly seven hundred miles some salmon will travel from the Pacific to Stolle Meadows, their birthplace and that of the South Fork of the Salmon River, where they will spawn. They begin the trip about now and will arrive sometime in July—during the hottest time of the year. To know summer on the South Fork, I spent a week, not far from Stolle Meadows, backpacking along her shore. The temperatures were in excess of one hundred degrees. My companions and I would rise early to walk in the coolest part of the day, and at night, we would sleep on top of our bags, wishing the stars were rain, wishing for the slightest breeze to cool our skins. During the day we took our books and lunches and bunched in a narrow stream drainage where we kept our feet in the water, cooled our heads under a short pour off, soaked our hats and clothes in the cooler water of Fritzer Creek only to have all of it parched within an hour.

The winter before had been a dry one. There were fires throughout the west, and smoke was our unfortunate companion that only seemed to intensify the heat. It was on that trip, working the nozzle of my water filter between rocks, that I saw the first dead sculpin. I turned to my friend, a fisheries biologist, who stood a few feet behind me just as she noticed the dead fish. I watched as a look of shocked sadness and then exasperation passed like a cloud across her face. She pointed a finger longer than the fish itself, a being who despite their constancy in the river, stayed hidden, camouflaged, pressed against the river bottom without a bladder to give it buoyancy, and said, they are the river's thermometers. Seeking a reading we would understand, we tied my backpack thermometer to a length of fishing line and sunk it in the water. A few minutes later, when we pulled it out, the reading was in the 70's. My friend got on her knees at the water's edge, saying over and over, *hot, it's too hot, too hot*, and shook her head as she looked into the water. Her stare dove past the reflection of sky, past what riffles remained, past the layer of thick, warm water, to the thin, only slightly cooler water below. She looked for salmon, not just with the eyes of a scientist, but with the look of a child who knew that something was wrong and that somehow they'd played a part in it. It's a look of regret and apology, one I've seen in in the face of so many beloveds when they felt they were the cause of some hurt, some agony, be it from accidentally spilling their milk to the moment just after killing a deer. It's a look that says *My god, what have I done.* Salmon cannot survive in a river with a temperature this high.

Is prayer a refugia? Though here I think it is important to point out the subtle difference between refugia and refuge, as subtle differences matter to the former. Whereas refuge as defined in Webster's Ninth New Collegiate Dictionary is "a place that provides shelter or protection from danger or distress" or "something to which one has recourse in difficulty," refugia, in contrast, is defined as "a geographical region that has remained unaltered by a climatic change (such as glaciation) affecting surrounding regions and that therefore forms a haven for relict fauna and flora." What gives me pause in that sentence is the juxtaposition of "climatic change" and "haven," but the word that stops me altogether is "relict" which adjectively means widowed, but whose noun form represents plant and animal species living in isolation in a small, localized area as survivors from an earlier period or as what's left of a nearly extinct group.

My heart wanders to another friend who is with us, whose ancestors fished this river for salmon for thousands of years. I hear their voices in her prayers and stories. If it is the words that land between hands or are cast on water when we fear the losing of something loved, something beloved, of life itself, then prayer is merely refuge and the refugia we beg is in the hands themselves. I lift the marooned sculpin from the sand and walk it out into the shallow water. When I place my cupped hands in the water then open them, the sculpin sinks almost immediately from my view, its work done, as if the river itself had sent a plea, a prayer to the feeble gods who have some power to save. As if it is trying to empower with a different godliness, as if the river has hope, hope in, of all things, us.

Today there is neither abundance of heat nor sunshine. It's been weeks of this and it's not so much the snow anymore as the moroseness that has settled in. I have been reckless, as of late, attaching my emotions to seasons. Thinking I will be happier if I just hold out for change. I recall a bouquet of tulips sent by my late husband and a card that read, "Hold on. Spring is coming." But with it I became a relict myself. When I needed shelter from the pain of losing him, I went to the winter memories and found it. What bliss in naivete, but who could have known and how would I have changed the outcome when it is only my choices I control? There is some science that proves the need for sun to lift the spirits, but there's science, too, that proves perspective is power. Rather than waiting for the warmer days that eventually I, too, will want relief from, I find I have grown nonjudgmental of the weather and more interested in experiencing the days as they come, aligning myself with the will of the weather, moving through my days purposefully, trying to learn the song I am meant to sing, the one that carries tones of love, fear, regret, and apathy, in its lines, the one that defines me as human, just as the newly-arrived Cassin's Finches and robins sing songs belonging just to them. Let it be that, though, that brings me joy, their simple act of being, and not what I attach to it. Let it be the birds themselves who I will miss should they never again return and not that which I have projected on them, not a burden that is not theirs to carry. Let it be the salmon I am thinking of when I see the snow, let it be their convenience I am praying for, not mine. Help me remember that the promise of a better future lies in my actions, not theirs.

Two weeks ago, Caleb, the dogs, and I went down the mountain to Hells Canyon. We went to greet the season. To touch the skin of the earth, to see the colors the canyon held and hear the voices carried on her winds. Of a sunny morning we decided to take a walk along the Snake River, below Hells Canyon Dam. It felt good to see the multiplicity of color. There were purple Shooting Stars and yellow Meadow Buttercup. The green of the moss that clung to the granite was the mother of the green that was worn by the Maidenhair Fern. On the rocky cliffs across the river we spotted what looked like piles of snow but was piles of white fur on the thick bodies of Mountain Goat. I removed my winter layers and let the sun bring out my colors, too. I followed the blue line of water to where it led to the mouth of the canyon and there the sunlight spilled across the water, strengthening the surface and for a moment seemed like a silver trail we could walk. Blue were the lines that were riffles around rock. Blue was the sky where it met the walls of the gorge which rose unbelievably high. Green were the pine that were staggered intermittently, sojourners on this selfsame walk. And in the distance, the Seven Devils and, blanketing their flanks and peaks, snow. Mountains and mountains of snow. There is the spring we seek, there in the mind of winter, and the language written in the cold water are theirs and the words, the message they carry is of hope.

The snow has started again in earnest. Little fists of snow. Snow like kisses blown in the air and frozen. Snow in clumps as big as some of the smallest chickadees. Snow that with a little more sun will begin to melt, and that water, as if desperate to return to its source, will start the journey down. Maybe some of this snow that I have watched all season will make its way to the Snake River, past the place where my family and I walked. Past where runoff seeped from a granite wall, where I pressed my face against moss until my nose and cheeks were so cold they hurt. Past the place where, after we turned away from the snow-packed mountains, turned back toward the dam, I saw the silver semi backing down to the river, its belly full of young Salmon, its presence shadowed by the very contraption that created it. It backed up and a hose was placed in the water and a valve opened and thousands of young fish entered the water. I tried to find them in the current, but the river is a good mother, covering her own, and all I could see was cold water. Only water. Just like now, only snow. So much snow it seems that there has always been and will forever be snow. And though it does not seem possible, I no longer seem to mind, maybe the river's desires have also become mine, for if rivers could hope, this would be theirs.

Love,
CMarie

"Letter Born of a Snowy Morning" was begun as letter to my friend Laura Pritchett and is therefore dedicated to her and the hope we try to inspire in one another and our students.

Gallinas River Park:
Rules and Regulations

by
Leeanna Torres

*P*osted rules at the entryway to Gallinas River Park in Las Vegas, New Mexico, are intentional and real. But the sign they're on is fading; the wood is cracked, the words hard to read. Each rule is painted in green, while the background, a fading white.

Last summer's rains through this part of Nuevo Mexico were thunderous and violent, their impacts downstream intensified by upstream wildfires. Ash and dirt compounded the river's flows, their signs seen far above the creek's average waterline.

Beneath the river park's posted rules sign, I wonder at the lawlessness of water in the changing landscape around us.

NO ALCOHOLIC BEVERAGES

Early September, just three days past my birthday—nine years sober.

"To thine own self be true" invites the saying printed on celebratory coins, including mine, hidden in a pants pocket. All along the Gallinas Creek, fall is beginning to show: the cottonwoods green leaves lean into yellow and a bright patch of yerba del manzo is in full bloom. While my work truck waits in the gravel parking lot just off National Avenue, I walk along the river park, trying to listen for the sound of water behind traffic.

At last, agua. And the sound of cars fades.

At the creek's edge, I watch the water, listen to the tone of prayer in its subtle trickle. A text comes through on my phone. It's my grand-sponsor, Kate. "Happy birthday, one day at a time!" reads her text, and I am grateful for both water and friend.

Along the narrow asphalt pathway, there are a few empty beer cans. Along the creek and among the willow and alamo, there are plastic miniatures, glass pints; they are always empty of course, always drained down to the last sip.

At the water's edge, water slowly trickles around stones and sticks, a dragonfly flirting along the surface. But this creek is prone to flooding when conditions are right; when thunderous water rushes downwards off the mountains to the north, the landscape and everything within it is violently transformed.

There are floodwalls, sandbags, retention blocks, all current technology to stabilize creek banks and control erosion. Along the trail, remnants of sandbags lay against the light-blue temporary retention walls between the creek and residential businesses and homes.

The truth is, despite all efforts and funding, we cannot prevent nor fully protect the Gallinas from flooding. We can only reduce the impacts, develop solutions that will salve, but never fully solve.

It is just like sobriety, all of it fragile. The scent of yerba del manzo is subtle, as the season slowly leans into change.

ANIMALS NOT PERMITTED TO RUN
AT LARGE ON PUBLIC PROPERTY

An afternoon breeze, and the sound of rustling cottonwood leaves. A woman walks her dog. A man with a backpack. Rumble of a diesel truck along the main highway and over the bridge. This creek, this river—the Gallinas—winding through the heart of a rural New Mexico mountain town. What keeps it alive? I think of rain, the common monsoons of summer becoming more and more infrequent.

I visit this river park whenever I pass through on Interstate-25. Turn off Exit 345, then drive straight on University Avenue to the heart of Las Vegas, New Mexico. My parents met here while attending Highlands University in the sixties. I, too, attended college in this town, but never finished. I'm sad I didn't come to *this* river *more* while as a freshman in college. The river could have been, should have been, a sanctuary.

Now, decades later, I'm surprised by the rio's subtle, almost hidden presence in the heart of this small New Mexico town.

In the summer of 2022, the Hermits Peak-Calf Canyon Fire devastated the mountain lands. Then, late summer monsoon rains arrived, raging across the fire-scarred land, flooding the town, flooding the watershed.

A woman walking her dog rests at one of the picnic tables alongside the river park trail. From the small pouch at her waist, she takes out a treat for the dog, hands it to him only after he sits. She lets him off-leash, and he takes off down toward the creek, toward the water, sniffing all along the way. She's scrolling on her phone now, eyes off the dog. He takes a dump near a small shrub, between a cottonwood and a Siberian elm, before sprinting away, off to sniff something else. The woman is distracted, doesn't see the waste her dog left behind.

What rules did the US Forest Service not follow when they started prescribed fires, even though conditions were dry and the winds were wild? What rules didn't they follow as the fires burned out of control, scorching, destroying, killing more than 340,000 acres of lands? And what rules do *we* not follow as responsible stewards of our *own* lands and waters?

I look to one of the cottonwoods, its towering and overlooked magnificence. It's probably fifty to one hundred years old. I wonder about the rest of September, and all it will and will not bring.

NO BIKE RIDING OR SKATEBOARDING

A Native man walking along the river trail says he's from Zuni Pueblo, and is selling jewelry. He shows me a bracelet, then a set of earrings. "They're real silver," he says. But when he hands me the bracelet, the metal is thin and light. The man doesn't seem shady or shiesty, and when I offer a polite "No, thank you," he smiles and simply says "Okay." He sits at one of the river benches further downstream, setting his bicycle behind him, leaning it against the bench like an old horse.

Here in our state, with reservoirs nearly empty, aquifers declining, rivers drying, irrigation ditches mostly empty, and forests burning, a Native man offers to sell me jewelry. He's just trying to make it in this world, and I wonder how long he's had his bicycle with its torn seat and bent front rim. He's just trying to make it in this world, like the rest of us.

He leans and rests on the bench as though he's about to take a nap, easy and calm, and his broken-down bike leans just as easy, and I wonder how many miles he's put on that bike, and what other river trails he knows?

On social media, New Mexico Outdoor Recreation posts this: "Northern New Mexico's Rio Gallinas has been ranked ninth in a list of the most endangered rivers in the US." The nonprofit group American Rivers has named the Rio Gallinas among America's Most Endangered Rivers, most notably for the consequences of the Hermits Peak-Calf Canyon Fire and the Forest Service's outdated protocols for forest management, prescribed burning, and watershed management.

It's midday, this river park is quiet of people except for the two of us. We sit under the shade of the trees along this creek, he with his jewelry and bicycle, I with a pocket full of unanswered questions.

NO CHILDREN UNDER SEVEN YEARS WITHOUT AN ADULT

At the edge of the Gallinas River, a woman wears a black coat, hood over her head, tennis shoes on her feet. Beneath her long cotton skirt, her legs are skinny. She holds a Catholic-liturgy-book in one hand, and talks, either via Bluetooth or to herself. "Michael, shut the fuck up, I *told* you not to keep bringing up his name, 'cause there's nothing I can do about it . . ." She rants and passes by, her pace steady.

On a red brick building between the river corridor lined with alamos, willows, and olive shrubs and the parking lot, a sign reads "Rainbow Road Therapies Inc." All three windows on the store-front-side are barred with black iron rods. On one side, river park, on the other, city and town. They exist simultaneously. Which will endure?

Last summer when the flood waters came, the people of Las Vegas braced for the worst. How high did the floodwaters reach along this building? The bars can keep thieves from breaking in, can keep riffraff from contemplating shenanigans, but are useless against water.

I think of the dangers of this creek and its waters. Would I allow my own little boy to play along this path alone, even in daylight? Along with raging floodwaters, there are other dangers, as well. I imagine shadow figures who walk this park, intentions unknown.

But it is a public space, where danger and solace intertwine. Rather than live in fear, I choose to walk along the paths of the river.

CITY OF LAS VEGAS NOT RESPONSIBLE FOR ACCIDENTS IN PARK AREA

The cookies from Charlie's Spic & Span (the beloved local bakery and restaurant) are safe inside a white paper sack, similar to one that might be used to pack up vodka miniatures, or a pair of doughnuts.

With my white paper sack of a half-dozen cookies (yes, I said half-dozen cookies), I head down to Gallinas River Park. Seems I'm always just passing through this town, but I always make it a point to stop. In fact, I *make* time to stop, lured by bakery cookies and the small río that is the Gallinas.

The Gallinas Creek flows from the Sangre de Cristo mountains, southeast of Elk Mountain, and into Las Vegas, where it becomes the Gallinas River. After that, it continues flowing southeast to join the Pecos River six miles northwest of Colonias. Early Hispanic settlers called this by its full name, Rio de las Gallinas.

The town of Las Vegas was founded in 1794, and in 1829, a military report referred to the area as Begas de las Gallinas. Sometimes people just called it Las Gallinas, but the name that survived is Las Vegas.

This Spanish word Gallina can mean chicken or hen, but in New Mexico, it usually refers to the gallina de la tierra, the wild turkey.

A squeaky bicycle passes by, ridden by a young man in shorts and a cap. His tee-shirt sleeves are cut off; he looks fresco but in a hurry.

The green of the alamo leaves is different from the green of the elm leaves. The foxtails along the banks are even another shade of green. Agua santa runs through this creek, and to hear it passing downstream along boulders and rocks is to listen to the sound of summer itself.

Charlie's Spic & Span is packed to the brim this June Monday morning. The whole community is coming out of the pandemic. Every booth and table is full, and a line of patrons wait for a table, and the bakery cashier's line is full, too.

"You guys always this busy on a Monday afternoon?" asks a Chicano man wearing a Hawaiian shirt and a boot on his leg, as though he might have broken a toe. The cashier answers him, "Oh yeah," and the man is surprised: "Ahhh laaa!"

Down by the river it is quieter. There is space to hold my breath and think. Or pray. Or just enjoy cookies and coffee.

Why do I keep stopping here on my visits through this town? Why does it continue to be an important place?

Instead of searching for answers, I enjoy the cookies. Appreciate the pink and white frosting Spic & Span chose today, a lovely sugary combination, and I break a piece and dunk it into my coffee mug. It's a momentary joy, so small, just like the stream flowing just on the other side, agua santa.

PARK HOURS:
6:00 a.m. to 10:30 p.m. WEEKDAYS
6:00 a.m. to 12:00 p.m. WEEKENDS

This río, this creek, becomes river, and eventually joins with the

Pecos River, which in turn flows into the Rio Grande. This merging of water, this becoming, all begins first with springs and creeks, and there is something about these smaller beginnings of water that makes me think about our own fragile humanity.

On the fifth day of December, I sit and write inside Charlie's Spic & Span. There is something settling about routine: visit Spic & Span and then visit Gallinas Creek River Park. This has become the smallest, most private ritual. "Cookies and café, please," I order from the bakery counter. After this I will go down to the ríto, to the river park, and the rules will be there on the fading sign, like they have been for years. At the end of the day, who follows these arbitrary and unenforceable rules? I return to this place, this park, this trail, to be near the water, to hear its flow, to witness its movement, and each time, the sign of these posted rules that seem silly.

Are they silly or do they make me uneasy?

These rules are posted to keep people safe. They are rules for order and cleanliness. But who came up with these rules? Why are they listed alphabetical instead of numbered? What is the Spanish word for rules? I search my own vocabulary, trying to remember. Instead, the only word I find, again and again when returning to this place is simply agua.

I think about this new normal we live with, the looming reality of less water in the American West, less and less.

Along the Gallinas River, there are flood walls and stone gabions; man-made inventions to tame the wildness of water. The wild of water.

What rules do waters live by? What rules do landscapes follow or dismiss? Or are waters and landscapes lawless, as roaming and rowdy as humans?

For me, these rules and regulations have come to stand for reflection, a meditation, an observation of water, the ríto itself. And this *place* has become both experience and repose, a place where I observe not only the landscape and ríto itself—a system—but also the *people* who are drawn to this river park, too. Characters and wanderers, those up to no good and those who could care less. Just like me, they come to this river park, each for their own reasons. Sometimes following the rules. Sometimes not.

Sitting at the edge of a creek with a notebook and a white bag full of pastries, I think of the drought. I think of fire, and of ash and sediment, and then of rains and floods. I think of people and rules and daily living along landscapes close to water for survival, for sustainment, and even for pleasure. But water is wild, just as we humans are wild, and we are set to no rules, no matter how they are posted. Because here is the incredible and final rule: there is no finality to contain the wild, the tameless. La agua.

Sade in the Pandemic

by
Fatima van Hattum

They dug a tunnel
under the Continental Divide, shifted
the course of a river, moved
a mountain range, water
meant to flow into
the Pacific now finds itself
in the Atlantic, no wonder
things feel so disoriented.

I am in the wilderness
You are in the music
In the man's car next to me

Yesterday, I passed a teenager
on the three-point line, in the heat,
right arm rod straight
in the air, hand crooked at the wrist
didn't need to see the ball
his face and perfect hand, rapture
for a moment we can forget the
loss, dancing in a crowd, sweating
in unison, mindlessly licking
someone's ice cream cone for a taste
of their flavor. The lake has become

a river again, original curves and
contours visible, even waters meant
for the Pacific cannot push this river,
the dryness just keeps flooding and
flooding. I am in the wilderness, you
are in the motion in the boy's hand
next to me. We are in a tunnel of
disoriented water beneath a continental
divide, unsure to which ocean we
belong. We are in a river that
became a lake and is a river once again.

We are in the wilderness.

Rillito

by
Ruxandra Guidi

Sometimes I live near a river. It's the Rillito, or "little river" in Spanish, an ephemeral one that carries water only when it rains or when the snow in the Catalina Mountains melts. Most of the year, the Rillito is a dried-up wash where mesquite trees and tall grasses grow; at dusk, I often see coyotes running between the bushes, or people walking their dogs in the riverbed.

But the Rillito didn't always look this way. About a century ago, the flow was continuous and the riverbed was lined by bigger, more water-dependent vegetation like willows and cottonwood trees. As regional agriculture and the city of Tucson grew, groundwater pumping destroyed the perennial stream and with it, most of its riparian habitat. What once was a "little river" would widen with each flood, becoming a raging force that was unleashed each time it rained. To try to control it, a channel was built.

When I moved to the desert four years ago, seeking a steady home after a decade of moves lasting no more than a couple years each—Los Angeles, Quito, Ecuador, Austin, La Paz, Bolivia, Boston—I had no appreciation for that dried up wash, for all that comes with even a little water, from bugs to flowers to tadpoles, regardless of the season.

Last winter, water came down nonstop for days so our Rillito brimmed with life. Just west of us in Southern California, my former home, an atmospheric river brought with it storms, flooding, and landslides, killing dozens of people. Such is modern-day life in the West:

Nature's disrupted cycles can mean an early bloom or late freeze, and also a frustrating commute or, at worst, a death sentence.

It didn't need to be this way.

The forces of nature weren't always this destructive, this often.

But also, we were never meant to be this disconnected from its pulses.

Across geography and culture, our ancestors had greater reverence for nature's myriad expressions every day: what makes a river swell, or how a forest landscape regenerates after fire, drawing insects to feast on the burned plant matter, and, in turn, becoming food for other animals. As a city dweller living in Tucson far away from my cultural roots in Caracas, Venezuela, a dense urban area that's at least five times Tucson's size, I find myself searching for this deeper understanding of the nature around me and how it shapes and nurtures all of us.

I'm not the only one seeking meaning these days. And I'm not referring to fuzzy, abstract feel-goodness that works like a pill might for a bad headache. I'm talking about a sense of duty to the landscapes around me, of being able to see myself like the tiny and insignificant creature that I am, dependent on a complex ecosystem. I'm referring to the ability to slow my frantic pace, to make the time to see the world around me. To grasp its meaning—not just for me, now, but for all of us.

Anthropologists call this animism, from the Latin word anima, or soul, a concept that may be as difficult to decipher as dreams, death or apparitions. Animism also has a problematic history. The founder of cultural anthropology, Sir Edward Burnett Tylor, first introduced the word in his work *Primitive Culture* from 1871, arguing that culture progresses from primitive to modern expressions. Today, Burnett Tylor's theories are considered beyond anachronistic: They project dangerous stereotypes onto Indigenous peoples, denigrating their worldviews as childish and backward.

Before colonization—and with it, the accelerated spread of organized religion—such worldviews guided us to listen to the natural world, to move with its beat. For many people around the world, these songs never stopped playing. Others from various cultural traditions are learning to listen to them anew.

"That desire is real because it is a part of us as humans," Quynn Red Mountain told me when I met them recently at a park in Tucson. "And people are looking for it." Their name, Red Mountain, is in reference to their father, a tall redhead who earned the nickname in his youth.

A 55-year-old white woman originally from Portland, Red Mountain calls themselves an animist minister for Web of Life Animist Church, a church "for Earth-honoring people" that was legally founded in 2008. They are quick to correct me: Animism is not a religion but a practice, a set of beliefs and actions that honor the original way humans connected with each other and with nature before those relationships were distorted by modern religions and ways of life.

I first heard of Red Mountain on social media: "Water Gratitude Walk on the Santa Cruz River, 1 p.m.," the post read. I showed up at a park by the Santa Cruz, the other intermittent river flanking the city. I was curious to feel the gratitude I recognize when I'm outside, but which, in the company of strangers, turns to wariness of joining a woo-woo New Age gathering. Four others who seemed as unknowing as myself came, too. "I just figured it'd be nice to be outside with other people," a woman I met in the parking lot told me. She looked like she was in her forties, like me. "I'd grown used to being alone during the pandemic."

Red Mountain gave a brief overview of landscape restoration efforts that are bringing treated wastewater back to this section of the Santa Cruz River, allowing it to flow sporadically and with it, bring small fish and amphibians. Then everyone walked along the riverbed, chatting side-by-side while occasionally picking up trash.

"My ancestry is not from here, so I tread carefully and don't assume any kind of knowledge," Red Mountain said, describing themselves as just a visitor to Tucson, which is one of the oldest continually inhabited areas in North America. The idea for the river visit to the

Santa Cruz was simply to call people's attention to its regeneration in such a short amount of time, Red Mountain explained, to say "thank you for this water that is helping the animals and this place."

In my head, I tried saying "thank you" too, skeptical of who, if anybody, would be listening.

I am an atheist, and I don't think we need a God or gods to have a deep respect for all living things. Does my godlessness mean I'm incapable of feeling connected? I refuse to think so. Witnessing anthropogenic change and recognizing my own role in it has been disorienting and sad; I'm not looking for a magic pill that will keep me from feeling this pain. Instead, what I'm searching for is the kind of guidance my grandmothers or great-grandmothers would have given me had we had more time together.

A global movement over the last six decades around "shamanism" has often been driven by non-Indigenous peoples. But a collective gratitude for nature and its inherent magic need not be in the form of Indigenous appropriation, says Natalie Avalos, an Assistant Professor in the Ethnic Studies department at the University of Colorado Boulder.

People are demoralized and alienated by modern-day lifestyles centered around materialism, technology, productivity. "I think a lot of people of European descent in the US, settlers that were disconnected from their own land-based traditions, have had a real sense of grief and have felt the allure of the New Age movement," Avalos told me.

Though many New Age adherents romanticize Indigeneity, today some of these people are also starting to develop a political consciousness defining boundaries around appropriation. In spiritual circles, Indigenous leaders have long been asking non-Indigenous peoples to recognize their white privilege, to understand that the ecological crisis is deeply tattered to colonialism.

"I'm genuinely surprised," Avalos, a Chicana scholar of Apache descent, said of this growing trend. "People have started to connect the dots more, but we still have a long way to go."

"What do you do about the white folks who want to capture Indigenous spirituality to find meaning?" she'd ask Indigenous leaders in her ethnographic research. "Go to your own traditions and recover those. Try to draw on your own ancestral European traditions," they would tell her.

The way Avalos sees it, there is a sincere effort within European descendent communities who want to change the way they relate to life, to land, and "model new ways of being in the world for other white folks."

This modeling of new ways is necessary: it can influence mainstream consciousness, and eventually change how white people and marginalized, especially Indigenous, peoples relate to one another. "We have to start somewhere," she said.

Almost two hours southwest of Tucson is Baboquivari Peak, a 7,730 foot-tall mountain that's sacred to the Tohono O'odham Nation and peppered with forests of forty-foot-tall, centuries-old saguaros, a species that the Tohono O'odham people revere, too. This is the home of the creator, I'itoi, who lives in a cave below the base of the mountain. According to tribal narratives, Baboquivari is the bellybutton of the world—where the earth opened up in the very beginning and humans emerged after a great flood. From within his cave in Baboquivari Mountain, I'itoi still watches over his people.

Tohono O'odham people regularly make pilgrimages to the cave and leave offerings for I'itoi. But the peak is in the hands of the US Bureau of Land Management, and since the late 1990s, the Tohono O'odham Nation has been actively trying to reclaim the sacred mountain as part of their reservation. Returning those lands would not just honor Tohono O'odham traditions and worldview, it would guarantee Baboquivari's care into the future.

Inspired by similar Land Back efforts around the world, a movement known as "new animism" is building consciousness about nature and the rights of its various life forms—whether rivers or trees or mountains like Baboquivari. In many ways, new animism is prompting us to unlearn the Western view that nature is separate from us and no more than a collection of resources to be extracted and exploited. New animism wants us to ask: What if we secured the same rights for nonhuman beings as we do for people, but through legal means? What if we revert to a pre-industrial view of nature?

This new animism may be a product of our collective climate anxiety, or the expression of a hope: That if we begin to see bodies of water or plants as fellow beings, we might learn to behave in more ecologically sustainable ways.

Or maybe, it's a sign of something much more basic and personal. I am learning to acknowledge the Rillito every time I pass by, reminding myself that it isn't just a wash, but a whole ecosystem. Maybe recognizing its unique cycles will help me see it—and us—anew.

Ocean Cactus

by
Santana Shorty

There are places where it is too warm
Where hurricane dust coats surfaces
so that when you sit down with your unAmerican coffee,
you must dust the tabletop, and it reminds you
the storm is coming

Island time is Indian time
There are no Indians here anymore, only this one who is a tourist
A cactus among the birds of paradise and accidental orchids loving
    on palm tree trunks
What happens when a cactus gets too much water?
There are no Indians here

Yesterday I passed a woman at the marina,
and her novelty shirt read
"My Indian Name is Falls Down Drunk"
I don't like the smell of rotting fish

In the water below, giant tarpon fish called to me,
inviting me to join them in this water that feels too warm
My torso stayed on land and I watched a man flush soap and bleach
    from his boat deck into the water and the tarpon sang louder
What happens when a cactus gets too much water?

"My Indian Name is Falls Down Drunk" woman doesn't wear sun-
    screen
She wants to be Brown and lays in the sun each day with her vodka
    sodas
Funny how Brown she wants to be
when there are no Indians here
The storm is coming

What We Talk About
When We Talk About Waters

by
Kate Schimel

On a late summer evening, I stood in the rain in the park near my house, waiting for the dog to pee and watching the waters that uncharacteristically filled the riprap-laden ditch that runs through the center of the park. They pushed the leaves and trash downstream, flowing around shopping carts and discarded appliances and nudging discarded clothes and garbage bags toward the river. I saw a coyote, patchy with mange, run along the edge of the waterway. Maybe the waters had disturbed its usual haunts in the ditch and forced it on to the banks.

Later that evening, my husband called to say the Santa Fe River was running.

Although its dammed upstream reaches provide the city with water, the river here is elusive. Downtown, it takes the form of a widely ignored ditch, a dozen feet below street level and a few feet wide. Hundreds of tourists likely walk beside it or drive above it without ever realizing they've forded the Santa Fe River. It's usually damp, sometimes trickling.

On our side of town, out where the trees fade and the small farms and working-class suburbs begin, the river is just a dry sandy cut between neighborhoods. But during the spring melt and the summer monsoons, officials sometimes let water pass its two dams in the hills above the city and the river rises from its subterranean groundwaters and flows. I've never seen it make it all the way to the Rio Grande, its final destination. But when it runs, we go see it, we say hi and touch the water and experience the thrill of watching a few inches of water push its way down the sand, around the occasional boulders, and past the suddenly shockingly green bushes that line its path.

We mark the seasons by the river's rare appearances and more common disappearances—its high summer form as a hot, dry strip of sand or its fall form, covered in branches and dead leaves. My husband found records that it once carried enough water in winter to ice skate on, but not anymore. To us, it's The River. However, legally, mercurial waterways like this one sit in a legal liminal space.

What is an official waterway? Can that term encompass paths across the landscape that are only occasionally wet? For decades federal courts and presidential administrations have decided yes and then no and then yes again. No one, not the courts or federal agencies like the US Environmental Protection Agency or the Army Corps of Engineers, can seem to resolve the question for good. In 2006, late Justice Antonin Scalia, writing the court's decision to limit the definition of a waterway, famously mocked the idea of water in the desert, detailing all the instances of lower courts upholding seemingly ludicrous water bodies. "Most implausibly," they'd supported treating as waterways "'washes and arroyos' of an 'arid development site,' located in the middle of the desert, through which 'water courses . . . during periods of heavy rain.'"

If you think legal opinions need to be sober and even-keeled, Scalia's shows the possibility for sarcastic, even scornful, legal analysis. It also showed the possibility for two people to have incredibly different life experiences. East Coast born and bred Justice Scalia clearly knew a kind of waterbody I had rarely encountered. And he never seemed to have met any of the rivers and creeks and arroyos I knew. His definition excluded my local ditch, of course, but likely also the Santa Fe River and much of the Los Angeles River watershed. It would also exclude about 90 percent of the water bodies in New Mexico, including ones that feed the state's agriculture, act as sites of worship, and offer a chance for a quick dunk during June hot spells.

One winter, when I lived in a small, dry farm town in western Colorado, my friend and I made a pact: We were going to swim in a wild body of water and ski every month of the year. But we were busy and our standards were low and we lived at the edge of the desert. Very quickly we began to interpret the terms of our promise far more loosely than Justice Scalia would have liked. We skied a lovely finger of snow in the mountains above town and then stripped in order to lie down in the four-inch-deep river—wild—that flowed out of it. If we could get our faces under, my friend reasoned, it counted. We accomplished this by lying face down until we ran out of breath—swimming. Once we were dressed and warm, we drove back to town where the river tapered to a small sliver of frozen water that wound between mud and rocks.

By the end of the year, I'd mostly skied a dirty patch of snow thirty minutes outside of town and one hundred yards long. And we'd done most of our "swimming" in an agricultural ditch that ran behind my friend's house. Reading Scalia's scorn for the now-you-see-them-now-you-don't nature of arid waterways, I think about those two unimpressive, ephemeral bodies of water transforming how I connect with the places we live.

The ditch we relied on for our summer swims feeds roughly fifteen thousand acres of farms and ranches. It was carved into the hillside relatively recently, first as a small conduit for river water and later as one for water from the Paonia Reservoir, built upstream in the 1950s. Each fall, we'd watch it fade into a corridor of mud and dead plants when water from the reservoir stopped flowing. Then, each spring, we'd see the same mud-laden creature return, its murky waters flowing the same slow-moving path each year, with the same concrete-channeled patterns. When it eventually dries up from the sedimentation filling the reservoir or a nasty fight over water rights, its lineage will have existed only a few decades, a bit more than a century.

The dirty snow patch, however, seemed like a new creature every year. It grew, lived, and died in the same ecosystem where it was born, the same ecosystem where every one of its ancestors had been born since long before the ditch was ever built. Its borders changed slightly from year to year and month to month. Sometimes it became a hard, icy rhombus tucked against the base of the cliff. Other times it softened, warmed by the sun, and sprawled across the meadow, pock-marked with grasses pushing through. And in the high months of summer, it left an indentation filled with an unusually verdant swath of wildflowers. Each time I got ready to ski it, I felt a little nervous buzz. What surprises did it hold? What would it be like? Would it even still be there, or would it have migrated downstream into the reservoir, to rest for the winter, before flowing through the concrete-lined ditch?

In his opinion, Justice Scalia argued that his definition of a body of water—flowing, big, always wet, never dry—was, ultimately, the only natural one, the one any reasonable, thinking person could agree to. It was simple, he seemed to say, this category is clear. It casts the world's topography as one of bounded things. A geographic feature, water, is one thing and not another, land. It's certainly not two things at once: wet and dry, there and not. And there's certainly a compelling human logic to it. Daily life is full of messy decisions; wouldn't it be nice if someone out there had a clear explanation and some order to impose on it?

But this logic is a kind of intellectual cheat code; it attempts to cut a straight path through what, in fact, is a labyrinth you have to steadily make your way through. It's not just water; most aspects of geography defy straightforward categorization. Don't think too long, for example, about what constitutes a mountain. And certainly don't raise that question with someone from another part of the country, unless you are looking for hours of debate. A category that includes the Appalachians and the Rockies, but excludes the Black Hills, is certainly not one with clear boundaries any reasonable person can easily define. I'm not saying you can't define these things, just that you might have to put up with a little more shiftiness than Justice Scalia seemed comfortable with.

I am trying out a wobbly definition of water these days. To me, a body of water is one that changes, that moves around and adapts to the weather, that has a life and a force of its own. It's the snow patch, adapting its shape to temperature and sun angle and precipitation. It's the Santa Fe River, unexpectedly flowing in February when the snows melt too quickly, or in August when the monsoons come, or like this spring, during a big snow year and a wet spring and the whole town comments on it. The river is flowing. That's what makes a body of water.

Skinny-Dipping

by
Luke Runyon

One of the first times I ever felt truly at peace in my body was when I stood naked on a rocky Wyoming cliff.

It was a clear-blue day in the summer of 2016, barely warm enough to even consider skinny-dipping in a high mountain lake. With nothing on but my Chaco sandals and a red bandana tied around my neck, I peered down the ledge into a crystalline lake more than twenty-five feet below.

A small lump grew inside my throat. I had just peeled off my shorts and T-shirt, following the lead of the man I was dating who had brought me to this place. We left our clothes in a pile between a lichen-covered boulder and a patch of Indian paintbrush.

He had already leapt from the cliff and was treading water below me.

"Are you going to jump?" he shouted up.

"Just taking it all in," I called back.

I was eager to impress. We met the winter before and I fell hard. At the time, he was living in Laramie, and I was an hour south in Fort Collins, Colorado. He grew up in Wyoming, at the base of the Tetons. When I met him, he was rugged and hirsute, wore Wrangler jeans. Sometimes he would trim his beard down to a mustache. A few years earlier he worked for a summer at a dude ranch. Very Broke-back Mountain. And to go along with that buckwild spirit, he seemed always ready to jump off cliffs into rivers or lakes, naked or not. No convincing needed.

I'm from Illinois, and my Midwestern upbringing has left me more risk averse. I need time to make up my mind—whether for a big life decision or a small one, like leaping naked into a lake. I can get there eventually, once I realize how lame I'll look for not doing it.

"Any day now," he hollered.

On our first few dates his spontaneity felt like a glass of cold water to the face, in a good way. I had been on the dating scene for years. Dozens of first dates. Few seconds. No one had excited me like Dylan.

The lake where we decided to camp for the weekend sat due west of Laramie in the Snowy Range, at the end of a muddy, nearly impassable Forest Service road.

We had only been dating a few months at this point. A couple weeks before our trip to this tiny alpine lake, he took me on an off-trail hike in the foothills above the sleepy outpost of Woods Landing. Halfway through he asked if I wanted to hike naked, to really take in those nature vibes. My face flushed and I demurred.

"Oh, uh, I think I'm ok, but you go ahead," I said. And he did. He walked naked through sagebrush fields, while I, like a chump, meandered down the hillside fully clothed. By the end I wished I felt as free as he did. Even here, dozens of miles away from the nearest town, I worried about being seen. In hindsight, that makes no sense. If there is one place on this planet you can get away with hiking naked and not run into another soul, it's probably southwestern Wyoming.

It's not that he was some hardcore nudist, nor that I was some stuffy prude. We were still in that phase of testing each other a bit. What feels comfortable? What's too much? What's not enough? What can the other handle? Dylan likes to push the envelope, and in this case, to push the body-conscious man he was dating to let go and live a little.

Which is why, when he gave me another chance to do just that at this tiny alpine lake west of Laramie, I knew I had to.

I grew up as one of the fat kids in class. During my most impressionable years, I hated my body. I'd wear baggy sweatshirts, husky-sized jeans and avoid places where I was expected to shed layers.

Swimming at the pool in summer meant keeping clothes on to conceal what I didn't want anyone else to see. I wore an oversized shirt when in the water. "It's so I don't sunburn," I'd tell other kids. But even they knew.

Locker rooms were particularly anxiety-inducing. All four years of high school I skipped the showers after P.E., and each time would change back into my school uniform, all sweaty from class. Stinking all afternoon was apparently better than giving jocks mockery fodder.

I was always a little too fat and a little too gay to fit in at my high school. I had friends but was far from popular. My weight turned me into a wallflower—less likely to say yes to things. I was more comfortable at home, and off on the sidelines. An observer, not a participant.

That shy, self-conscious teenager feels completely different from who I am now. Coming out as gay at twenty years old, in my junior year of college, allowed me to fully embrace who I was, both the inside and outside. Slowly but surely, my body began to feel less like something I needed to hide and more something I wanted to show off.

By the time I met Dylan in my mid-20s, and he opened my eyes to the wonders of skinny-dipping, I was feeling much more at home in myself.

I'll pause here to say this: Skinny-dipping can feel like one of the most luxurious experiences on Earth.

Whether in a cloudy, sediment laden river or a clear, blue alpine lake or a shallow, cobblestone hot spring, immersing in water makes me come alive.

In my day job I cover water issues across the Colorado River basin for a network of public radio stations. It is easy as a journalist to get sucked into the bureaucratic systems built to manage the region's limited waters. The inter- and intrastate politics are fascinating to me. It's what keeps me engaged and coming back to the beat day after day.

For many of the sources I talk to, the West's rivers and lakes exist in a conceptual world of paper water, split and distributed among an expansive cast of characters, to irrigate hay fields and flow through kitchen faucets. In my swims, I remind myself they also exist in a physical, tangible space—where their waters slick hairy torsos, drip from fingertips, pool in belly buttons, and form rivulets on the smalls of backs.

Swimming naked is now a year-round activity for me, even in the Rocky Mountains. There's a hot spring in northern Wyoming only accessible by skis in winter. By midseason, the steamy creekside pool is ringed with feet of snow. Taking off clothes becomes an intricately choreographed act to avoid plunging bare feet into snow, or dunking ski pants into the water. I've nearly thrown out my back just trying to stay upright.

Dylan and I have been together for more than seven years, and I'm almost sure that our swims have pulled us closer. Our love grows stronger the more adventures we take, the more we push each other to take leaps of faith, either literal or figurative.

We've stripped down to swim in river eddies, at hot springs, in frigid creeks with waterfalls, in the Colorado River and many of its tributaries. We swim by ourselves. We swim with strangers around. We've even goaded friends into becoming our fellow skinny-dippers. The ranks of naked swimmers are growing, at least in our little corner of the world.

Sometimes, swimming naked is our entire destination. We've been on backpacking trips, hiking miles uphill, just to reach a lake for a midday swim, to let the water dissolve the sweaty salt deposits that ring our heads. Or we'll drive for an hour and a half to the developed, clothing-optional hot springs not far from our house to spend a Saturday chatting up legions of other skinny-dippers.

These days, if I'm not swimming naked when in nature, I feel like I'm doing it wrong.

• • •

For me, the whole naked swimming journey really took off in that summer of 2016, standing on the cliff above the shimmering Wyoming lake.

While I surveyed the water below, my sandals gripped the edge. A good ten minutes had passed since Dylan jumped. He climbed ashore to towel off, and we were no longer alone.

A woman with a long gray braid and bright-orange life jacket sat in a kayak across the lake. There was enough distance between us I'm sure she couldn't make out too much detail, and I didn't see any binoculars, not that I would have ducked behind a boulder if she pulled out a pair.

I waved.

"Looks like you guys are having fun," she shouted back.

We *were* having fun. As I gathered up the courage to leap, and not turn around to put my clothes back on, I could feel a formative memory being imprinted in real-time: *This is the moment I'm going to learn to love skinny-dipping.*

As I took a few steps back to create enough runway for a launch off the ledge, I felt something change inside myself.

My body, with its skin wrapped in a warm breeze, was strong and good and ready to jump.

Contributors

Aaron A. Abeyta, a Colorado native, is the author of a novel and five collections of poetry. His work has received an American Book Award and the Colorado Book Award. Abeyta's latest book, *Ancestor of Fire*, is shortlisted for a Reading the West Book Award. He is the former Poet Laureate of Colorado's Western Slope, was a finalist for the 2019 Colorado Poet Laureate, and won the Governor's Creative Leadership Award for 2017. For eight years, Abeyta served as mayor of his hometown, Antonito, where he lives with his wife and their daughter. Together, the couple co-founded and co-direct The Justice and Heritage Academy, a school based on the three pillars of environmental, social, and food justice.

Chris La Tray is a Métis storyteller, a descendent of the Pembina Band of the mighty Red River of the North, and an enrolled member of the Little Shell Tribe of Chippewa Indians. He serves on the board for All Nations Health Center in Missoula—one of 41 Urban Indian Health Programs located throughout the United States—and on the advisory board for Swan Valley Connections in Condon. La Tray's third book, *Becoming Little Shell*, will be published by Milkweed Editions in Niibin, Summer, 2024. His first book, *One-Sentence Journal: Short Poems and Essays from the World at Large* won the 2018 Montana Book Award and a 2019 High Plains Book Award. He was selected by Montana Governor Greg Gianforte to serve as Montana State Poet Laureate for 2023–2025.

Christi Bode is an environmental filmmaker who has been telling stories about land and water throughout the Western US over the past decade. Bode's work has been supported by the Colorado Office of

Film, Television and Media, Rocky Mountain PBS, Colorado PBS 12, Water Education Colorado, and the University of Colorado's Water Desk. Her 2022 PBS documentary, *Farm to Faucet*, screened at the inaugural 2023 World Water Film Festival at the Columbia Climate School's Water Center in New York City. Today, Christi calls Southwest Colorado home with her husband and two dogs.

CMarie Fuhrman, a native of Colorado, grew up near Horsetooth Mountain and Rocky Mountain National Park. For over a decade, Fuhrman has found solace and inspiration in the serene surroundings of west-central Idaho, her current home. She is known for her works such as *Camped Beneath the Dam: Poems* and her contributions as a co-editor to the anthologies *Cascadia: Art, Ecology, and Poetry* and *Native Voices*, and her poetry and nonfiction have been published in *Emergence Magazine*, Terrain.org, and *Cutthroat, a Journal of the Arts*. At Western Colorado University, Fuhrman is Associate Director and Director of the Poetry Concentration in the Graduate Program for Creative Writing.

Daniel Rothberg is a former staff reporter for *The Nevada Independent*. His journalism on environmental issues has been published in *The New York Times*, *Sierra Magazine*, *Bloomberg* and *High Country News* and recognized by the Society of Environmental Journalists and SPJ Las Vegas. Since 2021, Daniel has presided over the Nevada Press Association. He lives in Reno, Nevada is currently writing a forthcoming book with Island Press on water in the Great Basin.

Desiree Loggins is from Sacramento, California and has a BA in Environmental Studies from the University of California, Santa Cruz. She graduated with a Masters of Science from the Geography and Environmental Studies program at the University of New Mexico where her thesis, *The Nature of Environmental Planning on the Carnue Land Grant*, received distinction. While enrolled at UNM, Loggins supported community-engaged research and mapping projects for the R.H. Mallory Center for Community Geography. Currently, she teaches Environmental Science at A:Shiwi College and lives in New Mexico in the Pueblo of Zuni with her partner, dogs, backyard chickens, and a beehive.

Fatima van Hattum has a PhD in Educational Thought and Sociocultural Studies from the University of New Mexico and works as Program Co-Director at New Mexico's statewide women's foundation. Her poetry has been featured in: *CALYX Journal*, *Chapter House Journal*, *apt*, *Portland Review*, and *New Moons: Contemporary Writing by North American Muslims*. Her academic writing and satirical comics have been published in: *Critical Inquiry in Language Studies*, *Intersections*, *Chicana/Latina Studies*, and *openDemocracy*. She is from Abiquiú, New Mexico, is Muslim, has a large, wonderful family, and a somewhat confusing background.

Kate Schimel is a writer and editor based in Santa Fe, New Mexico. She is currently the news and investigations editor at *High Country News*, a publication about and for the communities of the Western US. Her work covers land, environment, and cultural issues, and the deep power that stories hold.

Laura Paskus has reported on environmental issues in the US Southwest since 2002. She has worked for *High Country News*, *Tribal College Journal*, KUNM-FM, *New Mexico Political Report*, and *Capital & Main*, and currently, is a senior producer for NMPBS, where she hosts and produces the television show *Our Land: New Mexico's Environmental Past, Present, and Future*. Her book, *At the Precipice: New Mexico's Changing Climate*, published by University of New Mexico Press in 2020, won the New Mexico-Arizona Book Award for Nature/Environment.

Leeanna Torres is a native daughter of the American Southwest, a Nuevomexicana writer who has worked as an environmental professional throughout the West since 2001. Her essays have been published in numerous print and online anthologies, like *New Mexico Review* and the *Minding Nature Journal*. Interested in the intersection where the ordinary meets the Divine, she's always looking towards how natural facts reflect spiritual truths and exploring the interconnections among us all.

Luke Runyon is a journalist covering water and climate change in the Western US. He currently serves as co-director of The Water Desk at the University of Colorado's Center for Environmental Journalism. Runyon has spent his career in public media, reporting for KUNC, Harvest Public Media, Aspen Public Radio, and Illinois Public Radio. He is the current board president of the Society of Environmental Journalists and is a former Ted Scripps fellow at the University of Colorado. He lives with his husband, Dylan, in Grand Junction, Colorado.

Maria Lane is Professor of Geography and Environmental Studies at the University of New Mexico, where she was named a Presidential Teaching Fellow. She is the author of *Fluid Geographies* and *Geographies of Mars*, as well as numerous articles and book chapters. At UNM, she also directs the R.H. Mallory Center for Community Geography, which connects UNM researchers and students with community needs and priorities in New Mexico. Lane is a recent editor of the *Journal of Historical Geography*, current chair of the J.B. Jackson Book Prize award committee, and a member of the International Scientific Committee for the International Conference of Historical Geographers. She lives in Albuquerque with her husband and children.

Michelle Otero is the author of *Vessels: A Memoir of Borders, Bosque: Poems*, and the essay collection *Malinche's Daughter*. She served as Albuquerque Poet Laureate from 2018-2020 and co-edited *New Mexico Poetry Anthology 2023* and *22 Poems & a Prayer for El Paso*, a tribute to victims of the 2019 El Paso shooting and winner of a New Mexico-Arizona Book Award. A coach, community-based artist, and racial healing practitioner, she is the founder of ArteSana Creative Consulting, dedicated to creative expression and storytelling as the basis for organizational development and positive social change. Originally from Deming, New Mexico, Otero holds a BA in History from Harvard College and an MFA in creative writing from Vermont College.

Regina Lopez-Whiteskunk was born and raised in southwestern Colorado. She resides in Towaoc, Colorado, on the Ute Mountain Ute reservation. In October of 2013, she was elected to serve as a member of the Ute Mountain Ute Tribal Council. She is a former co-chair for the Bears Ears Inter-Tribal Coalition and education director for the Ute Indian Museum in Montrose, Colorado. Regina also serves on the on various board committees, including the Torrey House Press Board. Most recently, US Department of the Interior Secretary Deb Haaland appointed her to serve on the Bears Ears National Monument Management Advisory Committee. She is a contributor to *Edge of Morning: Native Voices Speak for Bears Ears* and other anthologies

Ruxandra Guidi is a native of Caracas, Venezuela and is currently based in Tucson, Arizona. Her reporting for public radio, podcasts, magazines, and multimedia outlets has taken her throughout the United States, the Caribbean, South and Central America, as well as Mexico and the US-Mexico border region. Currently, Guidi is the president of the board of Homelands Productions, and a regular contributor to *High Country News*. She also serves on the board of *El Tímpano*, and, in 2018, she was awarded the Susan Tifft Fellowship for women in documentary and journalism by the Center for Documentary Studies at Duke University.

Santana Shorty is a writer and poet from northern New Mexico. She received her BA from Stanford University and is currently pursuing her MFA in Creative Writing from the Institute of American Indian Arts. Her work focuses on New Mexican landscape and culture, and multiracial upbringing and love. Her poetry was recently published in *Paperbark Literary Magazine* and *Identity Theory Literary Journal.* She is currently working on her first novel. She is a member of the Navajo Nation and lives in Albuquerque, New Mexico.

Sarah Gilman is a Washington state-based writer, illustrator, and editor who covers the environment, natural history, science, and place. She serves as a contributing editor at *Hakai* and *bioGraphic* magazines, and her written and illustrated work has appeared in *The Atlantic, Audubon Magazine, YES! Magazine, High Country News*, and others, as well as several books and anthologies. Sarah's work seeks to illuminate the complicated ways people relate to landscapes and other species.

Aaron A. Abeyta's "A Letter from the Confluence of a Very Old River" appeared in "Letters from the Headwaters" (2014, Western Press Books).

Versions of "When We Talk about Waters" by Kate Schimel and "Rillito" by Ruxandra Guidi appeared in High Country News.

"Water Eats, Earth Drinks" by Sarah Gilman is reprinted with permission from YES! Magazine.

TORREY HOUSE PRESS

Torrey House Press publishes books at the intersection of the literary arts and environmental advocacy. THP authors explore the diversity of human experiences and relationships with place. THP books create conversations about issues that concern the American West, landscape, literature, and the future of our ever-changing planet, inspiring action toward a more just world.

We believe that lively, contemporary literature is at the cutting edge of social change. We seek to inform, expand, and reshape the dialogue on environmental justice and stewardship for the natural world by elevating literary excellence from diverse voices.

Visit www.torreyhouse.org for reading group discussion guides, author interviews, and more.

As a 501(c)(3) nonprofit publisher, our work is made possible by generous donations from readers like you.

Torrey House Press is supported by Back of Beyond Books, The King's English Bookshop, Maria's Bookshop, the Jeffrey S. & Helen H. Cardon Foundation, the Lawrence T. Dee Janet T. Dee Foundation, the Sam & Diane Stewart Family Foundation, the Barker Foundation, Robert Aagard & Camille Bailey Aagard, Kif Augustine Adams & Stirling Adams, James Allen, Diana Allison, Karin Anderson, Richard Baker, Patti Baynham & Owen Baynham, Klaus Bielefeldt, Joe Breddan, Karen Buchi & Kenneth Buchi, Rose Chilcoat & Mark Franklin, Linc Cornell & Lois Cornell, Susan Cushman & Charlie Quimby, Lynn de Freitas & Patrick de Freitas, Pert Eilers, Betsy Gaines Quammen & David Quammen, Laurie Hilyer, Phyllis Hockett, Kirtly Parker Jones, Susan Markley, Kathleen Metcalf & Peter Metcalf, Donaree Neville & Douglas Neville, Katie Pearce, Marion S. Robinson, Molly Swonger, Shelby Tisdale, the Utah Division of Arts & Museums, Utah Humanities, the National Endowment for the Humanities, the National Endowment for the Arts, the Salt Lake City Arts Council, and Salt Lake County Zoo, Arts & Parks. Our thanks to individual donors, members, and the Torrey House Press board of directors for their valued support.

Join the Torrey House Press family and give today at
www.torreyhouse.org/give.